Did I Just

Kiss

the Waiter?

*To Stella,
with fondest memories of our
friendship in Atlanta.

Lee Cowan*

ISBN: 1-57502-104-8
Library of Congress Catalog Card Number: 95-096194
Copyright © 1994, 1995 Lee Carver

First Edition: November, 1994
Second Edition: October, 1995

Printed in the U.S. by
Morris Publishing
Kearney, Nebraska

Marketing Agent in the US:
Kelly Strohkirch
1368 High Site Drive, Apt. 105
Eagan, MN 55121

Feedback Solicited to
74361,1252@compuserve.com

Acknowledgements

Sandy Hutson Cuza charged into São Paulo and lit fires under a number of potential and fledgling writers. Without her instruction and enthusiasm, this book might still be languishing at ten thousand words and no sense of direction.

Mary Miller, freelance literary advisor, served again as reader before these words were released on the public.

Since these stories are far more than the Carver Family Chronicles, a warm thank-you goes to every person who was willing to share personal tales of the ex-pat experience.

To my husband Darrel
and our son and daughter, Quinn and Kelly,
without whom The Great Adventure
would never have happened

Table of Contents

Foreword

What is it that causes a person to want to leave his home country, sleep in hotels, live out of a suitcase, eat strange foods and bang his head against the Tower of Babel? Throwing him- or herself into the stew of global humanity, the "ex-pat" thrives on the constant stimulation of cross-cultural experiences.

It is necessary to define the word ex-pat because its modern usage is so completely different from the dictionary definition. Ex-pat: slang form taken from expatriate, which implies that one used to be a patriot, but no longer is, or has been banished from his home country. To the contrary, the modern business or diplomatic ex-pat is an export of his country's economic, technical, or diplomatic expertise, an emissary of modern capitalism. He or she earns a living as a citizen of the world. Rather than love our home countries less, we love them more, for we have seen the alternatives.

This book has been written to share the laughter of our best moments as ex-pats, and to further disseminate the misconception that all ex-pats are rich and live fascinating, exciting lives playing around the world while their servants scrub their floors and chauffeur them through the teeming masses.

Every story in this book is true. The names have been changed to protect the guilty—we who are willing to tell about the ridiculous situations we create, while living as ex-pats.

The Pedicure and Half a Driver

Life was very predictable in the small town where I grew up. You knew what was expected and what was acceptable in any situation. Excitement was rather hard to come by. Maybe that's why I always wanted to leave home and See The World. Or maybe it was only that I wanted to marry someone I hadn't gone to kindergarten with; someone who wasn't in my elementary school class the day I wet my pants from laughing at the story about the runaway monkey.

Whatever the reason, I wanted to travel. I wanted to see Paris before I forgot my college French. (I did, and discovered that I didn't know half as much French as I thought.)

When my husband was offered a position in Saudi Arabia in 1976, we accepted with a tremendous sense of adventure. We studied the religion, language, and culture, and flew—from my perspective—to the back side of the world.

That sense of adventure and a healthy sense of humor are essential assets for this kind of life. After arriving, we learned that a family had just "cut and run" having fulfilled only a few months of the agreed term. When asked to list the reasons, they wrote down six. The last was, "The wall-to-wall carpet has wrinkles." They were definitely in the wrong country.

Our family arrived in Riyadh having been told that a new house was waiting for us. That house wasn't finished for over a year after our arrival. After a week, the company located one apartment which was ready in a building that was being built, in a block of buildings under construction. We were the only residents in the whole area. There was no telephone, and there was almost no electrical power until night-time. Not even enough to run a television, and certainly not enough to power the window air conditioners. It was June, 115° F and getting hotter every day.

My husband Darrel had bought a one-year-old car from the owner of the dealership. He thought that meant it would be well maintained. Wrong! The dealer was quite wealthy, but he was a Bedouin and frequently lived in a tent. A goat had eaten half of an armrest, and the radiator had been filled with desert well water which turned to chewing gum in the engine. The dealer was selling it because it needed to be sold.

So Darrel left for work every day in his choking car. For a while, I had the two little children, no driver, no telephone or television, no air conditioning, and no outside play area. School was out, so most families had flown away for two or three months. The sense of adventure wore thin.

It was on one of these days that Darrel dashed in after work and asked if I had supper plans. We were having ground beef surprise over chopped corn cobs, so I quickly offered to put it away in the fridge if he had a better idea. He did. One of the families had invited all of us to their home for dinner. Yes!

I shook something out of the suitcase and threw it over my head while he put clean tee-shirts on both kids. We looked like homemade sin, but we were ready in five minutes. Air conditioning! Civilization!

I slipped on some nice wedge sandals, noticing the dry, cracked skin of my feet. They looked like I had been walking the desert behind a camel caravan. I took off the shoes and quickly brushed polish on the two toes of each foot that showed, put the shoes back on, and grabbed the kids and left.

And Darrel drove us to the home of the Yamamoto family, where the guests removed their shoes at the door before entering. Horribly embarrassed, feeling the whole world was snickering at my toes, I quickly made my way to the sofa

The Pedicure

with the thick, shaggy flokati carpet in front. I kept my toes dug into the sheep hair all evening.

The Yamamotos became our good friends, and we later lived in the same compound and shared a driver, as was company policy. They never mentioned my unusual pedicure the night we met.

This driver, Abdul, was a story unto himself. He was a native of Eritria, Africa, and had come for the good money in Saudi Arabia. He was unusually crafty, which eventually lost him the job, but we went through the jaws of death with Abdul for about two years.

Abdul was a product of his world, and as such, had limited regard for Masumi Yamamoto and I, since we were *only* Women. He took our instructions as suggestions and ad -

9

libbed from there. Since it is illegal for women to drive in Saudi Arabia, he was our link to the outside world. When that link got too rusty, Darrel had to explain, "Now look, Abdul. Lee is your boss. You work for her, not me. I don't need a driver." He took it kind of hard, but it helped for a while.

After all that work to learn Arabic, my driver and maid were Africans who spoke less Arabic than I, so we communicated in a mixture of Arabic and pigeon English. One conversation I remember well. Abdul picked me up in our car, when I expected him to be in the Yamamoto's car that day. I asked why, and he said, "Mr. Yamamoto car bloken."

Now Mr. Yamamoto had a master's degree from a superior American business school, but his English pronunciation lacked a certain *finesse*. Like many Japanese, he was not able to distinguish between the English "r" and "l." I explained this to Abdul, and finished off with, "Mr. Yamamoto's car is broken."

"Mr. Yamamoto car bloken," he stubbornly replied.

"But you see, Mr. Yamamoto always makes this mistake. English is my native language, and the word is pronounced 'broken.' "

Abdul's answer was straight-faced and tight-jawed: "Mr. Yamamoto man; you woman. Car bloken." End of argument.

It was near the end of our colorful relationship with Abdul that he was driving Darrel to work one morning when the inattentive driver behind them crunched out our tail light. All parties got out to look. In the other car was an executive of a client company of Darrel's, an Italian construction firm. He admitted his driver's fault, and readily agreed to pay for the damage.

"Just get it fixed," he suggested, "and send your driver to my office with the receipt. " There was no police report or anything legal, just a handshake between two gentlemen.

Abdul did as he was told, and soon presented the receipt at the client's office. The male secretary told him to be seated. He waited a very long time. Abdul tried several times to present the bill, but was treated rudely.

After several hours, the secretary went in to the executive, leaving the door open, and Abdul very clearly heard the executive say in Italian, "Now you can tell that fatherless African to come in here."

Abdul's home country, Eritria, had been an Italian colony just prior to World War II. Abdul spoke Italian fluently. We didn't know that, and this executive surely didn't know that.

Abdul came up off the office chair and exploded into the executive's office with a solid line of blue Italian streaming from his mouth. The executive rose behind his desk in a defensive stance, and Abdul's fists went up. Somehow, bloodshed was avoided, and Abdul was evicted without the money for which he had come.

The executive called Darrel, and Darrel talked to Abdul and got the other half of the story. Darrel called back, making an apology to avoid an international incident, when in fact our sympathies were with Abdul. A couple of days later, Abdul had to return to the Italian construction company for the check. It was ready.

There's just one more story about Abdul that has to be told. During the years that we had no telephone at the house in Riyadh, Darrel and I developed the practice of sending each other notes by the driver as he passed between office and home. Even after the phones were installed—and at first they were on a party line—we still often sent notes. Sometimes they were in sealed envelopes and sometimes not. But they were always closed with a sentimental three x's, representing kisses, above the signature.

Abdul had asked for a raise. He was already paid more than most drivers. We began to ask others what they were paying. Since each driver was shared by two families, lots of notes were flying around. These were definitely sealed in an envelope, although Abdul spoke little English and could not read English.

Unknown to us, Abdul was talking to another officer of the bank about driving for her, trying to get a better deal. She caught on, and sent a couple of notes to us as well. It was not her intent to hire him away from us.

Abdul realized he was in trouble, and might wind up with no job instead of working for the higher bidder. He got an employee of the bank, a fellow Eritrian, to help him write a note to Darrel. It was a stiff, formally worded note, comical in itself, explaining why he needed more money. And there at the bottom, he had signed it, "X X X, Abdul." He and his friend had been steaming open our notes over the teapot in the employee tearoom, translating the notes and devising Abdul's strategy. And that was the end of Abdul.

Six Miles Up

"Good eve'nin, there, ladies and gentlemen. This is your pilot, ol' Buck Trooper, speakin'. We just want ya'll to let us know if thar's anythang we can do to make ya'll more comfortable. We'll be flyin' higher and faster than you'd believe, so just sit back, relax, and enjoy the ride."

It is travel by airplane that makes ex-pat life possible as we know it. We load ourselves into metal tubes that are launched at 600 miles an hour. Strapped into seats while this tube bores holes in the sky six miles above the earth, we spend the time eating, drinking, reading, watching movies, and standing in line for a toilet. Ex-pats are given to complaining about air travel, but it is so far above the alternatives that we don't even consider transferring to a new continent by boat, or doing business in six South American countries in two weeks by train or car. Our lives are too compressed for any other means of travel. When we have a month of summer leave, we must go, visit, and return faster than is possible in any way other than air travel. But oh, the adventures we have!

I have a strong preference for the airlines of modern, developed countries. The sling-shot I sit in should be safely designed, maintained, and operated. Efficient ticket agents with phones and computers that work are also definite positive attributes. Also preferred is to have some shoulder room and be able to recline my tourist class seat by more than ten degrees, but getting there safely is the criterion on which I choose an airline. And while the cabin crew can speak any language they wish, it warms my heart to hear the pilot do his welcome in that Chuck Yeager drawl which American

Third World Air

pilots adopt, knowing that it implies that they, too, have the right stuff.

Confidence in flying is the name of the game—not like the feeling the passengers had when the state airline of a minor Middle Eastern country came to a screeching halt at the end of the runway just before going airborne in order to close the cabin door, which was standing wide open. The passengers craned their necks around to see what was happening. In addition to seeing the attendants struggling to close the door, they noticed that the tea bags had been looped by their strings around the galley doorknobs, drying out for use again later.

Dinner comes. In the Pacific, it may be something green wrapped in a banana leaf. Don't eat it. Improperly washed banana leaves are a major cause of food poisoning and the traveler's horror, cholera. Maybe dinner is a boiled egg on top of a large pile of white rice with some very hot red sauce poured on, all enclosed in a little paper box. Not what you would have ordered. You look at the food, evaluate how hungry you are, and try to guess what the chances are that this is going to make you wish you had gone hungry instead.

Our whole family was on a flight which landed in Cairo, Egypt, that didn't stop at the end of the runway. There was a line strung across the tarmac with some big rubber tires on it, as if this would help to stop a multi-ton airplane. The plane rolled over the line, one of the tires was ingested by an engine, and the air inside the plane suddenly smelled like burning rubber. We made a hasty exit with our knees wobbling.

It was also in Egypt that the boarding call was made and a human herd rose and stampeded the airplane. These were not Egyptians, but were impoverished workmen from another country who were leaving their homes and families to make a few cents a day in construction jobs in Saudi Arabia. Our son was trampled in the onrush, and my husband literally fought to pull him off the floor and into his arms.

I was not there. I was at the separate women's entrance being felt-up by a female guard. This kind of experience gives me a lot of patience with both assigned seating and electronic security checks.

Design of the interior of airplanes is so important to the convenience and safety of the passengers and crew. The specialty called human engineering seeks to plan every little detail to function easily and safely for humans. The cockpit of an airplane, for example, is created so that each button can be reached, each light seen, and nothing will be hit by accident. Even the passengers' bathrooms become engineering artistry as so many functions are fitted into a space almost too small to turn around in. My children and I have played out some fine dramas there when they needed assistance with bodily functions. Members of the Mile High Club, if there are any, must be accomplished contortionists, indeed.

It was in one of these cubicles that an anonymous male traveler had a unique accident. The breakfast trays had been cleared away as he flew to a conference in Chicago, and he felt the urge to go meditate in the tiny toilet. When the meditation was complete, he rose from the seated position, pulling up his pants so that he was bent forward and rising from a crouch. This put his head in contact with the wall in front of him, and the stewardess call button which stood out from that wall.

As he rose, the little plastic call button cut open the flesh of his head right at the receding hairline, and the gash of an inch or more spouted blood as only a head wound will. He struggled to hold tissue to the cut and simultaneously get his pants closed, rejecting the whole idea of passing out in the tiny room. Nothing was stopping the bleeding.

He got the door open and started down the aisle for a stewardess. She saw him coming with the bloody compresses on his head and rushed to his aid, eyes wide with fear. Airlines are afraid that a passenger will sue in a case like this, but all he wanted was to make sure his zipper was up and get to his conference in Chicago.

The beautiful young stewardess lavished him with attention, literally sitting with him, holding his hand and applying cold compresses to his head all the way to Chicago. The pilot radioed ahead and no less than an ambulance met him at the plane's door and whisked him away to a hospital. He was only a couple of hours late to the conference, and received a hero's welcome when he entered.

The scar has faded now. It's hardly noticeable. But if you ask about it, he may tell you he was once in an airplane accident. He won't tell you it was an airplane bathroom accident.

Air travel has become a lot more pleasant for non-smokers in recent years, but it wasn't long ago that a smoker might light up in a non-smoking seat, and few passengers or stewardesses would say anything about it. My friend Chris was flying to the U.S. from Japan when this happened, and that's a long haul in case you haven't noticed. She decided to clip this smoking thing in the bud.

Chris got the Japanese gentleman's attention and pointed to the "no smoking" sign over his seat. He pretended not to understand. She told him in English that he was in a non-smoking section, and he shrugged and said in Japanese that he didn't speak English.

Few Americans really learn to speak Japanese when they live there for just a few years, but Chris and her husband had determined that they would apply themselves to learning the language and culture during their stay. Chris, therefore, spoke fluently and precisely to the man in Japanese, telling him to put out his cigarette, he was in a non-smoking seat, and exactly what she would do if he refused. The startled man crushed out the cigarette and did not light another in that area for the rest of the journey.

You get to your seat on an airline, and right away the crew starts offering you a drink. Is it to create the atmosphere of hospitality and luxury, or to calm the nerves of "white knuckle passengers"? You've been running around with your tongue hanging out trying to get to the flight on time, and they want you to sit there and drink alcohol while the plane flies around at reduced oxygen and 10 % humidity. You get so thirsty, but an order for water "don't get no respect." You want whiskey? No problem. Coming right up. Water takes a half hour, and then comes warm in half cups.

"Sorry, I'm American. Could I have that over ice?"

It was the Islamic month of Ramadan in Saudi Arabia, in which worshipers do not drink or eat during the daylight hours. All alcohol is strictly outlawed in Saudi Arabia, but would be especially offensive during Ramadan. In the days that travel was done across the desert by camel, it was decreed that travelers did not have to abstain from eating and drinking during Ramadan, but should make up the fasting time later.

All religions have members who are not sincere in their faith, and will use loopholes to avoid adherence to inconvenient tenets. And although you'll never get an alcoholic drink on a Saudia flight, other airlines with routes in the area are allowed to serve alcohol after take-off. So it was that a British flight closed its doors, rolled down the runway, and almost as soon as the wheels were up, its cabin crew was in the aisles offering drinks. An Arab gentleman clothed in his native robe and headdress, the *thobe* and *gutra,* was eager to get a whiskey. As soon as he was served, however, a big hairy arm reached over his seat from behind and took away his whiskey. He got another, and the hairy arm returned and took it also.

He was furious, and rose to confront his unwanted censor. The big hairy arm's body stood up, and kept standing up far taller and larger than the thirsty Arab. With a thick Welsh accent he told the Arab, "You people won't let me drink in your country, so you can't drink in my airline." Every time the Arab got an alcoholic drink, the huge Welshman took it. The cabin crew chose to look the other way.

Did you ever try to get a good night's sleep on an airplane? Blinders, earplugs, an inflatable curved pillow, and an airline blanket help. When she was a pre-teen, our daughter came up with one more aid. We were living in Argentina, where she had become quite bilingual, and we were on the overnight flight to the U.S. She didn't have one of those "Do Not Disturb/No Molestar" stickers that can be placed on the seat, so she made her own. It said, "Do Not Molest Me." And no one did.

An airplane is one of those places where insecure people with money can act like bad children whose mothers didn't spank them enough. The air crew puts up with a lot from these boors. Recently an American actor, whose name and face you know well, felt that the first class flight attendant was not giving him the attention he deserved. He touched her hips, which attendants abhor, and asked, "Don't you know who I am?"

Without missing a beat, she turned to the other stewardess up front of the cabin, and said, "Julie, do you have the passenger roster? This one's forgotten who he is."

You meet a lot of different types on an airplane. We're hanging up there in the sky for hours, eating, sleeping, and living within a few inches of each other with no scene change and little action like a bad French play. The stranger assigned to sit beside you could be absolutely anyone, any type. Business people who travel a lot may seem to be antisocial. They take their seats without saying the expected niceties or introducing themselves. They've been burned before. If you never open that can of worms, you might get some work done, or catch a nap. Once you start talking, you may learn more than you care to know about this human being that fate has put in your air space.

A very attractive woman who traveled alone a lot and liked to work on airplanes was annoyed by male seatmates who persisted in trying to converse with her. She came up with those three little words that would give her the space she needed. She would look with great concern into the man's eyes, and ask, "Are you saved?"

Air travel used to be elite transportation. Not so anymore. In some countries, families can board with a goat or chicken. The total loss of all lives on a flight to Mecca in 1979 may have been caused by a pilgrim to Mecca who brewed tea over a charcoal fire during the flight. If so, he

19

had to have brought live coals onto the plane in his little brass warmer, perhaps concealed in his flowing robes.

My husband was traveling on a "no class" ticket and found that a laborer from an undeveloped country occupied the seat to his right. It was the longest hour and twenty minute flight he has ever taken. The man smelled like a goat, and was totally out of his element in the modern world.

There was no chance for communication after the standard greetings which cannot be adequately translated, but indicate that the parties are grateful to God for good health and wish each other well.

Never before nor since has Darrel been so overwhelmed with the coarse bodily functions of a stranger at his elbow. The young man apparently had a severe pulmonary health problem to which he gave vent without the benefit of a handkerchief. He repeatedly contaminated his seat and the back of the seat in front of him. Fortunately, no food was served on that flight, because no one near could have eaten and all would have been in greater danger of contamination if they had tried.

In personal contacts like this, which are not likely to happen to people who stay in the developed world, we are reminded of two burning truths: that man lives like an animal unless trained otherwise; and that we have done nothing to merit being born who we are. Our lives are undeserved gifts, and most people received a lesser gift than we.

Navy pilots have described flying as "hours and hours of boredom interspersed with moments of stark terror." Commercial pilots and air crews try to shield us from any awareness of danger, should it exist. They are not above outright lying about the reason for diverting a flight or returning to the airport they just left.

Darrel, who was a Navy Patrol Plane Commander before his present career, noted with interest that a pilot had said after take-off that we were returning to Miami as soon as we could dump fuel because a certain radio was out. He knew that the radio system named was little used and was also backed up by another system. Moreover, the passengers fell asleep within fifteen minutes, except our curious son who tried very hard to stay awake and reaped a massive headache.

After we had landed and the passengers were off the plane, Darrel chatted with the pilots and confirmed that the cabin pressurization was inoperative as was the intercom and several navigational radio systems.

I don't know about these things, and Darrel is not going to say anything to frighten me and the children. So my handy rule of thumb is this: If Darrel keeps reading his magazine or doing paperwork, all is well. If he looks anxious, can't concentrate, or does a white-knuckle act on the armrest, I start praying *hard*.

Once we were flying contentedly when Darrel happened to notice through the window to his left that there was a fuel leak from the wing. He called the stewardess, identified himself as a pilot, and got her to lean in close enough that he could speak very quietly and show her the problem. She calmly went to the captain, who sauntered back, greeting passengers and looking friendly as he came down the aisle.

The captain spoke to Darrel, then slipped into the seat between us and took a better look at the wing. They talked in low voices for a while, agreed that the leak was slow enough that they could continue as planned. He asked Darrel to keep an eye on the leak and let him know if it accelerated. It didn't, and we landed safely without any other passengers being aware.

Flights like these are good to have every once in a while. They give you something to say when you are greeted with, "How was your flight?"

They give you a fine appreciation for boredom.

Don't Leave Home Without It

What's the single most valuable document a traveler has? What one item proves his nationality, bears all entry and exit visas, in fact proves that he exists? The passport, naturally. He needs it to cross borders, cash checks, rent a place to live. He needs to carry it everywhere and yet never lose it. Later, when the traveler is better established in the new country, he can do most in-town procedures with a laminated, authenticated photocopy of the passport and/or whatever local document is issued by the foreign country in which he resides. But there will be no way to cross a national border without a passport.

The Taylor family had enjoyed a marvelous ten days traveling all over southern Germany on a vacation from Saudi Arabia. It was wintertime, and the Taylors bundled-up in their coats and hiked brief paths of the Black Forest. They sat in two-hundred-year old inns and sipped hot chocolate by roaring fires. When at last it was time to go to the Frankfurt airport, they looked wistfully at the fresh snow and longed to make a snowman on that last morning.

Mr. Taylor got his family to the airport even earlier than the two hours in advance which is required for international flights. He was the first in line. The baggage check-in went quickly, and the tickets were all in order. There was nothing to do but turn in the rental car and go through the passport check prior to boarding the plane. Rather than spend two hours with two young children in the Frankfurt airport, he surprised the family with a wonderful proposal: "Let's go back to that little park we just passed down the road and build a snowman!"

Mr. and Mrs. Taylor and the two squealing children went to the park and for about an hour and a half they built the most marvelous snowman they had ever seen. They got very cold, which is exciting in itself when one lives in Saudi Arabia. When the time came to return to the airport, they were ready to go. The trip was complete now.

It was after the rental car had been returned and the Taylors were about to go through passport control that the horrible thought began to form in Mr. Taylor's mind: he didn't know where the passports were. In his pockets? No. In his wife's coat pockets? No. In her purse? No. When everything had been thoroughly searched, the truth was obvious: the passports were in a certain suitcase which had been checked in hours before, with all the subsequent baggage behind and on top of it.

The Taylors couldn't leave without those passports, nor could they enter Saudi Arabia without them and the entry visas stamped inside. And if the passports went to Saudi, the Taylors would be in Germany until the passports were returned. They probably would not be able to check into a hotel without a passport, and they certainly could not cash traveler's checks. The whole family would be without clothing, toiletries and medicines. Mr. Taylor's face went white, and Mrs. Taylor had such a roaring in her ears that she sat down for fear of fainting.

The ticket agent confirmed that the bags were already on the plane, but the baggage handlers would see what they could do. An anxious hour passed while the Taylors counted the minutes until boarding. At the last moment Mr. Taylor was paged, the suitcase returned and frantically opened and the passports all retrieved! Quickly through passport control, running down the corridor, they were the last passengers on the plane before the doors closed and the wheels started to roll.

Sinking into the airplane seat, Mr. Taylor quietly informed his wife, "I gave the baggage guys all the Deutche marks we had left—about thirty dollars. It's a bargain compared to checking back into the hotel for a week." And she told me that he also said, "I feel like such a fool. Don't ever tell anyone about this!" You won't tell him I told, will you?

Our family had some very anxious moments in the good old U.S. of A. one summer. We were living in the Middle East and making our annual pilgrimage to our homeland and parents. It was our practice to put all the valuable documents in one black valise. Another carry-on bag contained toys, games, and drawing supplies for the children to use whiling away the hours in transport. In the Mobile, Alabama airport, after checking in and getting our boarding passes, the black valise was put into the toy bag just to reduce the number of pieces of carry-ons to keep up with. In the waiting lounge before boarding for Ft. Worth, our son was scrambling for a toy and pulled out the valise in order to better hunt for it. Yep, it got left. We were at about 15,000 feet and climbing when my husband uttered those blood-chilling words, "Where are the passports?"

When the system works right, though, it's so wonderful. We called the flight attendant, she had the pilot call back to Mobile, and we learned that the valise had been found. The same airline had another flight between those two cities just an hour later, so we simply waited an extra hour at the airport in Texas to receive our precious documents and several thousand dollars' worth of intercontinental airline tickets.

The lasting effect of this and several other passport incidents is that I have become emotionally sensitized to the question "Where are the passports?" or the more pointed "Do you have the passports?" I have a permanent request that these questions be avoided if possible, or asked in gentle, soothing tones when necessary. Anything else hits my heart with a shot of adrenaline and little white lights go off in my brain.

Please allow a little background information here unless you already know the territory: most countries require a visa to enter. Some countries require a visa to exit, too. A family may have an established residence in one of these countries, living and working for years, and have to get an exit visa stamped in the passport every time they go on vacation, travel for business, or suddenly get called home for an emergency. It usually takes a few days to get an exit visa, and the passenger is passport-less for a while. If the visa department is not working with efficiency, or if the underpaid visa officials require additional incentive to get around to doing a particular visa, it may take much longer. Any routine visa or passport request may require trips to some foul, crowded public building and several hours' wait through the procedural maze. Companies which prefer that their executives not waste their expensive time will hire "expediters" to go through all the steps which do not actually require the presence of the ex-pats' bodies.

There was a Swiss family living in a certain middle eastern country, and they were making plans to go home for a vacation. All the passports were sent by the company's expediter to the office for exit visas in plenty of time, and three of them were returned with exit visas. But days became weeks, and the father's passport was still out. Heat was applied to the expediter, but still nothing happened. Finally, with very few days to spare, the expediter admitted that the visa official had conceded that the father's passport was lost.

In a panic the father, Herr Breuger, went to the office himself. Dust was swirling about the hot room, flies swarmed and lit on every surface, and the applicants had never heard of the quaint foreign practice of forming a line. They pressed against the counter in a solid, shifting mass, and the one with the sharpest elbows got to be first. Eventually, Herr Breuger worked his way to the front, and stood leaning on the counter until he had a chance to state his problem.

It looked like a no-win situation, though. The man in charge admitted that the passport was lost, and they really couldn't do anything about giving him a visa until he applied for and received a new passport.

But wait. Swiss passports are red, and while Herr Breuger had been waiting, looking around in boredom, he had noticed a bit of red under the desk behind the counter. He convinced the bureaucrat to check it out, and HALLE-LUJAH! it was his lost passport. The visa official explained that they had put the passport under there to keep the uneven desk from wobbling, as if that made everything all right. He stamped the exit visa in the passport immediately, and as our happy Swiss friend turned to go, the official took another passport off the desk and put it under the wobbly leg. Do you wonder whose passport is there today?

If it is rare that a corporate foreigner goes to a foreign government office, it is even rarer that a woman should go. In some countries it would be offensive for a woman to be in a public room mixing with—even brushing against—men. If she is not offended for herself, the men may either be offended or may take the opportunity to "accidentally" touch her. So ex-pat women generally avoid such jobs if possible.

Carol, an American living in Bahrain, was trying to get entry visas for her parents to come visit her, and nothing had happened in a reasonable time. Bahrain was an English protectorate until 1972, so most government employees speak English as well as their native Arabic. Carol waited for some time outside the office of the official who could break the logjam and grant her parents' visas.

Finally, she was admitted into the office, where many people waited around the very busy man's desk. When he spotted her standing there in all her blondness, he very graciously asked her, in English, why she had come. She briefed him on the problem, and he was concerned because her request had not been granted already.

Just the Right Size

On his desk were very large "in" and "out" baskets filled with routine visa and passport requests. He called an assistant in and told him in Arabic to take the "in" and "out" baskets out of the office and hunt for her paperwork while he stalled her with pleasant chatter.

In a few minutes her application was brought in and stamped right away, and she was bid a kind farewell. He was happy to help her, but had been embarrassed to admit that her papers had been in the stack being ignored on his desk. He never knew that she spoke Arabic and understood his instructions to his assistant.

Two American citizens whom we shall call Laurie and Tim were living and working in Brazil when they decided to be married. They chose to marry in Brazil, which is a paperwork-intensive country. Things got complicated when Tim could not find his birth certificate. He had been born in the Belgian Congo, now Zaire, to a U.S. diplomat, so he wrote the U. S. State Department in Washington, D.C. for a copy of his birth certificate. The State Department sent him a fancy document, all signed and with a raised seal, but it said he had been born in Belgium. He tried again, and received an equally beautiful certificate declaring his birth to have been in Beliz. Having waited long enough, the sweethearts flew to the United States and got married. Two years later, Tim's mother found the original birth certificate in an old trunk. So Tim now has three very official birth certificates affirming that he was born to the same parents, on the same date, in three different countries.

Some of the places ex-pats live and work offer little in the way of week-end entertainment. Take Dubai, for example. One week-end diversion there is going "wadi-hopping": ex-pats pile into a worthy desert vehicle and drive across the sand from one oasis, or "wadi," to another. They just scope out the terrain and see whatever is to be seen.

It was on a Friday afternoon (translate "Friday" to "Sunday" in the week pattern) that the Benders and Glazers had been wadi-hopping when they were stopped by a border patrol—of the wrong country! They had accidentally run through the desert across the border into Oman, and were now on the wrong side without passports or any suitable identification. They were detained by the Omani border guards for six hours while they tried to talk their way home and generally waited with unthreatening patience. They were allowed one phone call to their embassy, but couldn't get any help because it was closed. When the Omanis finally decided to believe them and let them cross the border, the Dubai border guards held them for another two hours while they once again tried to convince the authorities that it was all a harmless accident.

There are places in the world where everything floats on a sea of paper. Not only are receipts and every form of verification required, but it becomes common to affirm a person's identity and permission or authority to accomplish any minor task.

For example, the Reverend Plummer went to a hospital in a major South American country to visit one of his sick parishioners. He had visited the sick for years, but on this day was asked for his *permission* do so.

Patiently he explained that he was the pastor of her church. Again he was asked for a paper which authorized him to visit in the name of that church. He was the pastor, the only pastor of her church, he explained, and it was understood that he had the right and, in fact, the duty to visit its members. But the hospital official needed a piece of paper.

Rev. Plummer graciously retreated to the church office, pulled out a piece of church letterhead stationery, and typed his own permission in fluent Spanish on the church typewriter. Then he signed it himself and stamped it with three various stamps in different colors of ink—the date in blue, the church's name in red, and whatever he could find in the secretary's desk drawer. He returned to the hospital with the "permission" letter in hand and was admitted without further question.

It was the Rev. Plummer himself who told this next story, which is amazingly creative: two men in his city, in the hot, tired after-hours of a long workday, had a car wreck. They got out unhurt, surveyed the damage, and exchanged information on their identities and insurance companies. Since it would have taken a long time to get policemen to the scene when no emergency existed, they agreed to just go home and call their insurance companies and settle the matter quietly.

When contacted, however, the insurance company of the first gentleman who called said that they couldn't process a claim without a police report given at the scene of the wreck. There was no way around this requirement.

Being a resourceful person, he called the other party in the wreck. They agreed to meet and carefully "wreck" again at exactly the same place, same time on the following day. Their cars came together with just the right amount of crunch for realism but no further danger. They called the police, waited and got the report, and filed for the insurance.

The only difficulty was keeping the residents of that area away from the police. They were so impressed with the coincidence that two identical cars had had the same sort of run-in on the same corner just the previous day!

Argentina experienced wholesale abduction and illegal placement of children during its "dirty war" years before the current democracy. Intensive travel documentation is still required for a minor child to travel alone or with only one parent.

We knew the laws and had the documentation, but we assumed that if the entire family was traveling together, and since there were no divorce or adoption complications, the valuable papers should stay at home in the safe. That was a bad idea anyway, since travel plans can suddenly change. But there we were at the Buenos Aires airport, trying to prove that these children who looked exactly like us both, bear our names and carry passports and visas which indicate that they were ours—really were ours. In desperation, we put our faces side by side. "See, she has my eyebrows and his dimples." The immigration officers were not impressed.

This was the day after the international school got out, and every seat on the plane but the toilet was fully booked. If we couldn't fly on that flight, it would be a week before we could get another ticket, and Darrel's vacation days were counting down. The passport agents knew they had us in a bind. They let us go into the waiting lounge at last, but then called Darrel back for a more private discussion of what would be necessary for us to board the plane.

Now it became clear that it was not really a question of parentage, but of how badly we wanted to start our family vacation that night. Two missionary families, friends of ours, were leaving on the same flight and were already waiting in the passenger lounge. When Darrel was called back, they asked me why. Then they began a quickly, quietly huddled prayer meeting, circling right there in the departure lounge.

Darrel and the agents were about to come to an understanding which involved the payment of a fine without a receipt. But a young missionary volunteer, who earned a little money as a sort of ground hostess of the airline, spotted the impromptu prayer meeting and asked what the problem was. She then went back to the passport control area. Breaking cheerfully into the tense scene, she asked if there were a problem, and could she help? Like the sudden fall of a house of cards, the agents broke away, said there was no problem and that Darrel could pass into the departure lounge (again). Within thirty seconds we boarded with great relief, having learned again a lesson that we thought we already knew well: whatever paperwork might possibly apply in the wildest stretch of the imagination, don't leave home without it!

Home Away from Home

It is absolutely not true that I was wearing only bra and panties when I put the breakfast tray out in the hallway of the hotel and the door locked behind me. Eda told everyone that, maybe because that is all she would have been wearing. But I am a very proper person. Besides, I don't have Eda's body.

I was in Singapore alone and had breakfast delivered by room service because it was included in the price of the room either way, and I had an early appointment. On the tray was a nicely printed card asking that I call room service for pick-up when I was finished with the tray. Well, the maid could have gotten rid of it later, but I took a moment to call as requested. The person answering then asked me to put the tray out in the hall. What a bother. Why didn't the card just say so? I did have most of my clothes on, though, regardless of what Eda told, and stepped into the hallway with the tray, the room door being somewhat recessed. I was bent over to the floor when the spring-loaded door sharply clicked behind me and locked.

At least there was an in-house telephone down by the elevators, so I didn't have to go to the grand lobby in minimal attire to report the situation. I mean, it's just not that kind of hotel. It was much too early for maids to be on the floor, but they sent a guard up with a walkie-talkie who waited with me for twenty minutes until someone came with a key card.

One of the pleasures of ex-pat life is staying in elegant hotels when traveling on company business. The firm never asks you to stay in a "no tell motel." We are expected to be safe and comfortable and be able to do business while lodged there. These hotels have excellent restaurants and guest services, and make for much more efficient and productive trips. Most of their employees enjoy meeting people and take pleasure in providing professional service. Only once have I checked into a hotel that the clerk acted as if he were personally against admitting me, but had been overruled in the committee decision. His nose was so high that he risked spraining it.

Even the best hotels aren't perfect. In a hotel of one of the finest chains in the world I was duly registered in and ushered with baggage to a room that had not been cleaned since the last guest. It was late at night, and the room had been overlooked somehow. The bellboy was so stunned that he sprinted out and left me and the bags in the dirty room.

The phone soon rang. I tentatively answered, and it was the front desk asking me to go to a certain guestroom on another floor, where someone would meet me with a key. The bellboy came running back and took my bags. He, I, and another bellboy met at the new room assignment, but the key card wouldn't open the door.

People were running and phoning as if a real emergency existed! I wasn't going to start swearing and biting people. I had just flown from Texas to Singapore, though, and I wanted a bath, a bed, and a dark room. It was all worked out in time, and the next day the hotel sent an enormous tray of luscious oriental fruits with their gracious note of apology. I ate some of the unusual lemon-flavored mango and broke out in an allergic rash for five days.

Hotel receptionists say they can tell when a guest approaches the desk if he/she is a "difficult character." Guests tend to return to the same hotel over the years if they are pleased, and certain guests have very strong reputations among the staff. Especially the younger staff members get very nervous when they hear that someone like Mr. Grizzly is checking onto the executive floor that day.

What happened was that Mr. Grizzly stepped off the elevator onto the executive floor, already ruffled over some detail, and snorted his way to the executive check-in desk. The handsome young gentleman whose fate it was to greet him was not trembling too badly. The express check-in process was all in order. The receptionist began his words of welcome but was interrupted by a growl from Mr. Grizzly to the effect that he would teach the young man how to speak to him in the next few days.

The receptionist came around the desk and spread his arms wide saying that he would be happy to assist the guest in any way—knocking over the silver bowl of hard candies on the desk. The bowl and candies bounced and clattered on the marble floor and down the two steps toward the elevator.

The rattle stopped, the guest's scowl broke into a belly laugh, and bellboys scrambled to pick up the bowl and candies. The staff escorted Mr. Grizzly to his room, coddled him in every foreseeable way, and started counting the hours until his departure.

It is surprising how ungrateful some guests can be. Another guest, when shown to his executive floor accommodations, snorted, "The suite is all right, but you know I don't like champagne. Take it away and bring me some wine and cheese." No one asked how they were supposed to know he didn't like champagne. They just whisked away the offending gift and replaced it with wine and cheese.

I asked a particularly beautiful single reservationist at a luxury hotel in Chile if she ever gets requests from male guests which are beyond the scope of her professional duties. She laughed and said that she had been told that the two previous women in her job had been fired for dating guests. She gets invitations to the south of France, to ski in Switzerland—"I could own the world," she said, still laughing. "I like to handle it in my own way, and be nice to the gentlemen. I tell them, 'Thank you very much for inviting me, but my boyfriend wouldn't like it if I accepted.' In fact, I don't have a boyfriend." Isn't it refreshing to find a glamorous young woman with high principles? No, I won't tell who or where.

The manager of an excellent hotel in Brazil now knows that he has heard it all. In an effort to prevent the presence of unwelcome females on the guest floors, any unaccompanied woman is required to check in at the security desk by the elevators. (That's unfair discrimination, I know, but a fact of life down here.) Security calls the guestroom she intends to visit and asks the resident if she may come to that room. However, a male guest recently walked in with a prostitute and escorted her to his room, an action which bypassed hotel security.

When he woke up the next morning, the hooker was gone as well as four hundred dollars and other valuables. The man called the manager and reported the theft, expecting the hotel's insurance policy to cover the loss. Informed that such occurrences could not be covered under the hotel's policy, he became irate. The manager wisely suggested that the guest call his wife in Chicago and explain the situation to her, and have her file for the loss under their homeowner's policy.

In Brazil's major cities, motels are not primarily places for weary travelers to get a good night's sleep. They are for quick afternoon and evening meetings between two people who are not married, and the names of the motels leave no doubt as to their market position: Motel Quick, Motel True Love, even Motel Erotic, to name a few.

Our American executive friend was not aware of this, however, in his first few weeks here. He asked an attractive Brazilian woman to accompany him to a party at a home on the beach a couple of hours' drive away. She gladly accepted and they took off that Friday night and got lost on the way. He spotted a motel and darted in to ask directions without explaining his intentions to his date. The check-in and -out procedure is conveniently done at a little drive-by booth, without the guest having to get out of the car. He would just pull up there and ask questions. Odd, he thought, that so many cars are leaving the motel at this early hour. What's more, as his headlights shined on the exiting cars, all the occupants ducked.

Meanwhile, his date was stunned that he had told her they were going to a beach party on their first date, and now he was pulling into a motel before they got to the beach area. And he hadn't even asked her!

Hotels, like airlines, place you under the influence of lots of strangers. Here's a mathematical probability question: If a hotel has ten floors and thirty rooms per floor, how many of the guests are smoking in bed on any given night? I used to lie awake wondering how many bedsheets I would have to tie together to climb out the window and get to the ground in case of a hotel fire. Finally the awful-awful happened at 1:40 a.m. in Washington, D.C. The alarms all went off and the front desk confirmed by an open telephone line that there did *seem* to be a fire on the third floor. We were advised to evacuate the building. (Were we all going to "seem" to burn up?) I grabbed a housecoat and started out the door, but my husband was sitting on the side of the bed groggily putting on his shoes and socks.

"*Honey*, the place is on *fire!*" I fairly screamed. "You're just sitting there putting on your shoes and socks?"

This man can not be rattled. With a slight edge to his voice, he replied, "Well, I'm not going to walk through the flames in my bare feet." That sounded reasonable, so I grabbed my shoes and walked down fourteen flights of concrete service stairs with them in my hands.

The hotel was not on fire. Some rowdies had thought it fun to set off the sprinklers and ruin the third floor of a good hotel and a large part of the second floor as the water seeped down. The fire trucks came and everyone was out on the lawn for three hours in the middle of the night. The personal effects of the third floor guests were hopelessly flooded. The only positive result was that, having lived through the non-fire, I ceased to worry about hotel fires. That may not make any sense, but it's the truth.

In the summer of 1994 I traveled to attend the wedding of a lovely niece in the United States. In the same hotel were many members of the extended family. Apparently there was something wrong with the fire alarm in the hotel, because it went off a number of times. Stumbling down the back stairway in the middle of the night, I was trying to assist my arthritic aunt when I was walking no better than she. A few steps in front of us, however, the mother of the bride floated down the stairs wearing a beautiful peignoir accented with a gold necklace, gold bracelets, and her usual complement of diamond rings.

Later, as we trooped back up to our rooms, I told her, "I feel like a hag, coming out among all these strangers in the night wearing a cotton housecoat."

"I know what you mean," she replied. "We've been in so many hotel fire false alarms that before we go to bed in a hotel, I lay out my peignoir, my gold jewelry and hair brush. Then, if there's an alarm during the night, I'm prepared." This is the same lady who once told me that she never accepts an impromptu invitation unless she has at least four hours to prepare her hair, make-up and wardrobe. She's the frosting on the family cake. And one day, she may be the most elegantly dressed casualty in a hotel fire.

Darrel was traveling with a business associate to Mexico City on business a few years ago. Since the men would be arriving after midnight, they made guaranteed reservations and got the reservation number. The fax clearly stated their flight number and arrival time, just to be sure that the rooms would be held for them. Upon their arrival, however, the desk clerk said that the hotel was full. He admitted having made the guaranteed reservations, and that the credit card had been charged for the rooms.

He said he would try to find rooms in another hotel, but was unsuccessful and soon quit trying. Darrel insisted on speaking with the manager, which visibly upset the desk clerk. Meanwhile, Darrel camped out in the lobby with his boss, who had never been out of the United States before. In the wee hours of the morning, the bleary-eyed assistant manager stumbled downstairs, obviously awakened at Darrel's repeated request. He confirmed that the hotel was full. There were no rooms available.

Fortunately, Darrel had just finished reading the book You Can Negotiate Anything, and he remembered a ploy by its author, Herb Cohen. He asked, "Do you mean that if the President of Mexico were to walk through that door right now, you wouldn't have a room for him?"

"Well, yes, we would have a room for the President," the assistant manager admitted.

"I've got news for you," Darrel replied. "It's three a.m. and he's not coming. We'll take his room."

In fact, the men were escorted to the honeymoon suite with pink plastic flowers and hearts everywhere and a big round bed. They fell exhausted into the bed for what little was left of the night, and awoke in time for their 9 a.m. appointment the next morning.

While they were gone, the hotel moved them to very nice (separate) suites for the rest of the stay at no extra charge. The bottom line to negotiating is "never give up," and they had nowhere else to go.

For a really outlandish story, I must return to the Middle East. This happened in 1977, but the memory of our arrival in Riyadh is still clear. Sand like fine, gritty dust whirled around us as we stepped off the airplane into the searing heat. It was about four o'clock in the morning, and the fog in our brains cast an unreal quality over the experience. My husband's new boss came to meet us himself, and took us to a hotel.

"Your new house isn't ready yet, and the Intercontinental Hotel was booked up," he explained. "I've got you rooms at The Flower of the East." That sounded pretty good.

The first room to which we were taken was filthy. The second was a suite of sorts in a building behind the main hotel, at a cost of about $175 per night. The temperature was far, far over one hundred degrees Fahrenheit, but the hotel employee proudly started the rumbling, coughing air conditioners which were hanging precariously out of two windows. Faded red-orange curtains dropped from a rod attached on one side only. There was an old full-sized refrigerator that didn't work in a kitchen nook that spouted brown tap water. We slept in a lumpy old bed and there were two army cots for the children, who were young then. Only three hours later my husband went to his first day on the new job and an American couple took us into their home for a few days.

Don't ask the address of The Flower of the East Hotel for your next stay in Riyadh, though. The Flower has since died. The last time we passed by there, it had been replaced by a concrete fly-over intersection. The world is a better place for it.

A missionary to Brazil was traveling "in the interior," and stopped for the night at a hotel of the kind that he could afford—not a dump, but not luxurious. When he entered the room to which he was assigned and put down his bag, he was immediately aware of a heaviness of spirit about the room. Being a man of God, he was sensitive to such things.

The missionary bowed his head and prayed for any spirits of the adversary to depart. Instantly, every light bulb in the room burst!

Calmly, he went down to the front desk and asked for a new set of bulbs. Inquiring who had rented the room before him, he learned that a fortune teller had been there for a few days, and had practiced black magic with her clients. The missionary returned to the room and slept in peace, knowing that he was protected by a higher power.

Do you ever wonder who sees what on those little cameras mounted to the ceiling in hotel hallways? Mr. Singh, an Indian businessman, was in Singapore without his family for the weekend. He woke up late on a Saturday and decided to reach out, wearing only his briefs, and get his complimentary newspaper outside the door. No paper had been left at his door, but there was one at the door across the hall. No one was in the hall. A quick dash and he could snatch the paper without being seen. But as he grabbed it, his door shut and locked behind him.

Mr. Singh yanked at his door to no avail, and then cautiously made his way to the house phone by the bank of elevators. He explained his predicament, but to his embarrassment, they already knew. There was a camera that displayed the whole incident to the staff of the front desk below, and even recorded the newspaper theft to be played again and again.

A bellman was dispatched immediately to let him into his room, and Mr. Singh tried to put the event out of his memory. When he checked out the following day, though, the entire front desk crew waved and chuckled. As he walked out the front door, he overheard a bellman say, "Hey, look, that's the guy who..."

Foreign travel is a barrel of laughs.

Being Sick in a Foreign Language

Thirty Indonesians in a flooded paddy pulled against nets while others herded eels toward them. All the workers were bent over in knee-deep water, their bare feet slogging through the fertile mud. The equatorial sun beat on their wide straw hats and brown bodies as they harvested a sort of bonus crop of eels between plantings of rice.

Along the road to the side, but a world away, we ladies from an American charity group were bumping along in four wheel drive vehicles with our doctor-guide.

"Just look at those people laboring barefoot in that muddy water with no protection against disease," I said. "If we did that, we would be sick with dysentery and parasites."

"What makes you think they are healthy?" he asked.

The concept of health and well-being is so different in the developed world from what we live with in other countries, even fairly modern ones. We expect to be strong, to feel good, and to have diseases cured. Yet there are places where parasites and certain diseases are so common that being *without* them is unusual.

This doctor's wife had taken their little girls to the local pediatrician when one of them was very sick and weak, with frequent, cyclical sweats and high fever. The mother feared malaria, which many people suffer there. Her fears were confirmed, and she tried to discuss with the Indonesian doctor how to care for her daughter. He was nonchalant.

The mother questioned him urgently about malaria as if it were a problem, a disease to be seriously treated. Finally he interrupted her, saying, "Malaria is not a problem on

Sulawesi. About 90% of the people have it, but that's normal. It's not a problem."

The mother left with her daughters and sought help elsewhere for their debilitating, potentially deadly disease.

I was in Santiago de Chile gallivanting while my husband worked day and night. Clarita, the sister of a friend, was graciously showing me the city when an ambulance screamed down the street.

"Hospital of the Heart?" I asked, translating the big words painted in red on the side of the ambulance.

"Yes, it's a private hospital—for members only," she answered.

"Members of a heart hospital?" I needed clarification from Clarita.

"If you ever expect to have heart disease, you can buy a policy with that hospital. Then, if you have a heart attack, you can call them for an ambulance and treatment."

I've learned since then that it isn't an unusual concept in South America. Still, it raises a lot of questions. How many memberships do you need? Are there liver and kidney hospital memberships? What if you weren't expecting to have a heart attack?

In some countries, the educational process depends on sheer memorization rather than reason. However, the combination of logic and fact is particularly essential to diagnosing disease. Obviously, the riddle must be solved before it can be treated. It took nearly a year to diagnose excruciating, constant headaches in a certain woman in Jakarta. It was finally decided that there must be a brain tumor, so she went to Singapore for a CAT scan of the brain. When that test was negative, well, it had to be psychological.

Finally her daughter's art teacher at the international school, an Iranian woman who had the same disorder, told her for the third time, "You really need to consider the possibility that you are allergic to monosodium glutamate, MSG, which is in absolutely everything here. It's in the soy sauce. Cooks throw in solid MSG by the spoonful rather than salt. It's better known here by the brand name, Aji-No-Moto."

So she checked with her doctor, who said, "Well, sure, there's always that." And it was. Since she had a long history of migraines, that should have been the first thing to come to mind in Asia.

In certain countries, the doctors are so poorly paid that they routinely practice graft. The most common such practice does not injure the patient: a poor worker goes to a public hospital. The doctor receives only five dollars for the consultation, but he prescribes several medicines which are paid for by the patient's employer. The prescriptions are filled at the hospital pharmacy. A receipt is written by the doctor which falsely inflates the cost of the medicines, and the patient and doctor split the extra money.

In places where there is socialized medicine and all treatment is free, the more expensive treatment may be chosen whether it benefits the patient or not. The baby of my Brazilian *faschinera* (household employee who does floors, windows and heavier cleaning) was born by Caesarian section solely because she was "very old"—thirty. The baby was released from the hospital quickly, but she was kept for a week or so. The mother couldn't nurse her baby, and all manner of formula problems arose. Sadly, the first beautiful week of bonding was largely missed.

It would be quite unusual to receive better medical care abroad than at home, but it happened at least once. A man in his sixties was visiting his married son's family in Jakarta when he suddenly had a serious heart attack. He was rushed to a new cardiac hospital, and the problem was immediately and correctly diagnosed.

It happened that this hospital had received from the United States ten doses of a medicine which was designed, by a single injection, to dissolve clots in the heart arteries so effectively that the heart muscle would suffer little or no damage.

The reasoning of the emergency doctors might have been, "The Americans sent us ten doses to try out. This guy is American. Let's try it on him." They did, and the patient experienced a recovery that could only be described as miraculous. The irony is that he couldn't have received the American medicine in America, because it was not yet released there by the FDA.

Okay, let's see if we can lighten up this discussion. Part of the sea of paperwork in moving to a foreign country is proving that you are not diseased. Requirements vary, but it is typical to demonstrate an absence of venereal disease, AIDS, and alcohol or drug dependency.

Our dear friend who just moved to the Middle East wrote back the following vignette of his new life. To get a work permit for Egypt, after he had already arrived to live in Cairo, Paul was told to go to the leading hospital which treated foreigners. The company doctor also worked there and the hospital president was known. The company driver took him to a building so old that it seemed only the dust was holding it together.

After Paul tripped over the rug in the entrance, he confronted the open grill elevator, black and greasy and about the size of a truck. He was directed to an office, but the secretary there said he should go where the doctor was working. He was pointed out the back door into the courtyard, and down the alley to the doctor's office.

The building down the alley had only one door. Paul entered. It was very dark, so he stood a moment until his eyes adjusted. Blinking and waiting, he saw two feet under a sheet facing him. On a dolly, just inside the door, was a covered body. The only sound was the hollow, ghostly drip of water somewhere in the background. Paul had entered the hospital morgue.

Silently in the gloom, a man appeared and beckoned for Paul to go up the stairs of another building. Paul assumed he knew, then, what Paul was there for. He ended up in the dental surgeon's office. Paul determined that this hospital would draw his blood over his dead body. He left while he still could.

Darrel was in Peru recently for a three day business trip. Arriving at the airport for his return, one hour and forty minutes before the flight, he was told by the flight attendant at the gate that he had to have a yellow fever shot to return home to Brazil. For years he had carried his inoculation record with his passport and had never once needed it. This time he didn't have it.

To get the shot, he was instructed to leave the airport and go to a certain hospital which was only ten minutes away by taxi. There was a man waiting nearby for the purpose of earning a fee to help him get to the hospital. All his luggage was carry-on, including a notebook computer, so he hoofed it with the luggage to the far outer ring of the airport to which the taxis are restricted.

The helper put his bags into the trunk of a dilapidated, unmarked car and entered into a lively discussion with the driver and two of his associates in which a different hospital was named. As the argument heated up, Darrel started to retrieve himself and his bags from what appeared to be an unsafe situation. But they convinced him that all was well, and the driver was willing to take him to the destination named by the airline agent.

Arriving at the hospital, Darrel insisted that the driver wait to take him back to the airport as soon as he could get the shot. Nevertheless, he took his bags from the trunk. The driver seemed to expect this and helped him carry it into the hospital.

Once inside, Darrel filled out a form and paid in advance the fee of about twenty dollars for the yellow fever shot. Only one other passenger had come over from his flight. When Darrel started to fold the receipt, the reception-ist said he couldn't do that. At this point, Darrel was ready to take the man's head off, but the fellow just pointed to the waiting nurse and told him to give it to her.

The nurse stood in the tiny gray room, prepared to fight yellow fever back into the jungles. But she asked, "Do you want the shot?"

"I have to have it to return to Brazil," he answered.

"But most Brazilians are afraid of needles," said the nurse. "They pay the fee, but they don't want the shot."

So it was a legal rip-off. No one cared if he had been ex-posed to yellow fever. He didn't have to have the shot. He only had to pay for it. With the round trip taxi ride, it cost his company forty dollars; it cost him a last minute airport hassle and a personal invasion.

The nurse asked, "Are you Brazilian?"

"No, I'm American," Darrel answered.

"Oh, Americans are very brave. They always take the shot."

"Is the needle used only once and then discarded?" he needed to know.

She showed him the individually wrapped imported nee-dles and the sterilized serum bottle. He accepted the shot and watched her discard the needle.

Darrel re-dressed, raced for the waiting taxi, got to the airport on time, and returned home on schedule. He put his inoculation record with his passport before going to bed.

Then there was the time I took my fevered child to a family practitioner, an Indian woman, in Indonesia. Kelly's skin was hot and her reddened eyes glistened. The throat was swollen with a painful infection, causing a pounding headache. The doctor examined her quickly, and then said, "You're American. She drinks too much Coke. That's why her throat is infected."

In fact, soft drinks are not over-used at our house, and Coke doesn't cause children's throats to become infected.

Bacterial infections do. We refused ever to be treated by that person again.

Our home offices are quick to point out that hardship pay takes medical inconveniences into consideration. There are some experiences, though, for which money doesn't compensate. Like a mis-diagnosed ruptured appendix. My advice, not that it was requested, would be to always arrange to have your illnesses when you are back home. That's why we have vacations.

Business Class

Quite a few years ago, when my husband was a Navy pilot (same husband, different career), he and his crew were on an extended trip which included Taiwan. The flight was so long that there were two entire crews on board rotating flight duty. Exhausted and jet-lagged, they "crashed" in a hotel. Darrel was in his underwear headed for the shower when a bouncy young woman with a cheerleader smile entered with no embarrassment and no apology, saying, "Hi! I Wendy! I you social director! I arrange you shows, you nightclubs, you friends!"

He was too fatigued to be even remotely interested, and insisted that he did not want anything she had to offer. Over her jubilantly good-natured protests, he got her out of the room and locked the door.

After a few hours he woke up, stirred around groggily and found himself very hungry. He went out to dinner with some of the crew, returned fairly early, and undressed again. The door suddenly burst open without a knock, catching him again in his underwear. Another cutesie Taiwanese cheerleader type entered with no embarrassment and no apology, saying, "Hi! I Sandy! I you social director!"

"Oh, no, you're not!" replied the world-wise traveler. "I already know my social director. She's Wendy."

"Wendy you day-time social director," she countered. "I you night-time social director!"

She found it hard to believe that he didn't want to meet some girls, and he found it hard to get rid of her and go to bed, alone. Somehow he couldn't trust the social planning of a young woman who could stand there unabashedly trying to plan his activities with him in his underwear.

Many times during those years, people asked me how I could trust my husband when he was flying to cities well known for their ability to accommodate the needs of men. The truth is that a man who wishes to be unfaithful can do so in his home town. But what I usually replied then and still reply now is, "He leaves home satisfied. What more can I do?"

Business travel, to the uninitiated, sounds like getting a free vacation to an exciting other land. You have to have flown to Asia from New York City to know how far it is, what it feels like to lose twelve hours and never know what happened to Thursday, and how grueling it is to fly all night and work the next day. Too much is said in jest about business people who abuse an expense account and play with fire when traveling without their spouses. We are talking here about professionals who travel to do a task.

Some men, however, will take advantage of every opportunity. There were two men who ran their own partnership in a steel industry servicing company. They made frequent trips to the Minas Gerais area of northern Brazil. In this dusty outpost the warmest welcome, in their estimation, came from women-who-were-not-ladies who lived in a house a few kilometers from the steel plant. The distance to this house was not great, but it was up a steep, rocky, and rutted hillside road. The factory-owned car suffered so much expensive damage on the road that the factory paved the road to the house of ill repute as an economy measure. "And wide shall be the road that leadeth unto destruction."

But let us get on with the subject of actually working in a foreign environment.

Native English speakers have a definite advantage in business. When you hear business being conducted in other languages, the discourse is often shot through with directly adopted English terms for bookkeeping, engineering, or

Motel Strange Love

finance, such as "debit," "credit," and "wire transfer." It makes a lot of sense to use English terms when you consider, for example, that there is only one word for the totally opposite terms "payables" and "receivables" in Arabic. English words used in business dealings are more likely to be precise, legally defined terms.

Still, the executive may have difficulty being understood because the concepts involved in doing business don't always translate. Take for example the attempt to get a

51

"projected cash flow" from an Islamic businessman. The answer may be, "If Allah wills, I may be dead tomorrow."

Second try: "But if you are not dead, and the business is still operational, what do you think this year's projected cash flow might be?" Answer: "I cannot presume to say whether I will be blessed with disaster or great riches this year." And this is absolutely, totally correctly in line with his religion and his philosophy of life, but it doesn't give the account manager what he needs to approve a letter of credit or construction loan.

Extremely wealthy people will use any dodge to avoid giving a statement of their net worth. When pushed to the edge, if they still want to complete the negotiation, they may submit a statement which reveals a portion of their net worth which would satisfy the financial institution's requirements. If they want a $100 million loan, they reveal $200 million of their net worth. The rest is no one's business but theirs. The banker's axiom has been satisfied: Only loan money to clients who can prove that they don't need it.

In fact, just before the era of the multi-million dollar bank write-offs of loans to South America, The Buenos Aires Herald accurately reported the tirade of one Argentine *politico* who raved about how American banks only want to lend money to clients if they are absolutely sure of getting it all back, and receiving interest, too. Well, yes. That's the idea, isn't it?

Bankers routinely ask for the financial statement of a potential client. Some clients are happy to produce a financial statement which will state anything they perceive the banker wants to read. Occasionally, the client will ask, "What do you want it to say? Do you want it to show long term obligations, short term obligations, high leverage or low? How much do you need last year's profits to be?" The banker knows already that he/she will never get a figure from this guy which can be trusted. It may be time to close the briefcase and run.

Offers come for bribes, kick-backs, a little percentage into a separate account, or a gift for the spouse. These are acceptable ways of negotiating business in many cultures. It is shocking at first, and the uninitiated executive is caught off guard. He may fumble around trying to find ways to reject a bribe or kick-back without offending the client. His hesitation is taken as meaning that he is considering the offer, but he refuses it. Therefore, the offer is increased. Now he is really flustered, and begins to twist and re-cross his legs. He again refuses, so the client wonders how to make the offer acceptable. Maybe it needs to be more secretive. Maybe it should be jewelry or travel instead of cash. Or cash instead of a traceable deposit. The businessman quotes company policy, gets up smiling and shaking hands, and quickly leaves before another angle is attempted.

An honest businessman had just concluded a deal and the gentlemen relaxed into a few minutes of chit-chat. And that was when he opened his mouth wide enough to fit both feet in, and he said, "My wife and I have been wanting to visit your country on our next vacation. We've heard that the skiing in the Italian Alps is great."

This was taken as an invitation to the client to offer a little icing on the deal already structured in that session. They warmly volunteered that they would be happy to send tickets and resort accommodations for the whole family for any date that would be named. It took some serious back-peddling to get out of that one, but to his credit, he did.

There is another pitfall in international business coming up, but you won't be able to fix it this week: racial and national prejudices in the world go far beyond the familiar black-white and Arabic-Jewish categories. Koreans doing business in the Middle East are prejudiced against Pakistanis, and any nation known to eat dog meat is especially heathen to Arabs. Argentina has come a long way in recent years, but used to brag that it was the only white nation south of Canada. They killed off all their native Indians in campaigns by the 1800's, and have maintained a prejudice against people with any shade of dark skin. Remember, political correctness is a modern, Developed World concept.

You need a flow chart to determine racial pecking order in multi-national deals—not that you are going to play that game, but you may need to know the pitfalls created by those who do.

Mr. Carpenter was the executive in charge of a construction lending team in a major financial institution in Saudi Arabia. A Korean construction company won a bid on a large project, and wanted to do business with that particular financial institution. Mr. Carpenter assigned one of his finest young officers to the Korean company. This man happened to be Pakistani. The Korean company called and requested a change of account officers, but the request was tactfully declined.

Then an officer of the Korean construction company paid his respects to Mr. Carpenter and re-stated the request. He was told again that the Pakistani account officer was a superior performer, and besides, he was the only one in the department who could possibly take on another client. Next came a phone call inviting Mr. Carpenter to lunch with the regional director of the construction company.

It was no surprise that the director arrived twenty minutes late, since rules of "face" must be observed, but it did no good to the exchange to follow because Mr. Carpenter was always on a tight schedule. After the introductions and much posturing, the men finally sat down to the table. The senior of the three Koreans pulled a fat brown envelope out of his suit pocket and put it on the table without comment. They proceeded to order lunch.

In the dance of words which followed, the envelope was never directly mentioned, but the Korean senior made every possible suggestion that there was a way to change the Pakistani account officer for someone of a different nationality. Mr. Carpenter remained resolute. There was a tense pause while the two determined people burned eyeball to eyeball.

Then, as if comprehension had suddenly descended, the Korean exclaimed, "Oh, of course! I understand! What would your *wife* like?"

"There is nothing that my wife needs either. I cannot change your account officer, and I will not."

The Korean senior then flushed and steamed, stood up, put the brown envelope in his pocket, and left the restaurant without lunch. The remaining three had a very uncomfortable meal together.

It is obvious to the reader that the principle was more important to Mr. Carpenter than the potential profit. Those were the days in the late 1970's when forty percent of the construction in the whole world, by dollar value, was going on in Saudi Arabia. Mr. Carpenter's institution certainly got its share of the market. But the real surprise is that the Koreans did not go to another lender, of which there were many. The Pakistani became their account officer and finally won their confidence. More than a year later, the in-country senior officer of the Korean construction company conceded to Mr. Carpenter that the young Pakistani had done an excellent job for them.

Anyone dealing with large amounts of other people's money will be offered bribes. There is no need to even consider this a temptation. If the decision is made once and for all that bribes will never be accepted, then it doesn't matter when, where, or how much is offered. The answer is no. It makes life a lot easier to decide in advance and never look back.

Companies vary a lot in their policies concerning the payment of "facilitation fees" to foreign clients or potential partners. Some do not ever participate in this kind of deal, and others make it a matter of practice to do business the way that foreign clients expect it to be done.

Once that can of worms is opened, the most amazing things come wriggling out. It is an accepted practice, especially in the orient, to wine and dine clients with enormous expense accounts. Since "wining and dining" may also include women and gambling, one means of disguising a cash bribe would be to call it a poker loss in the process of entertaining the client.

A U.S. manufacturing executive working in South America recently told me that there is frequently a 1% "procurement fee" added to manufacturing contracts, which does not have to be justified by receipts. It is available for cash payments as needed to make the deal happen. A mere 1% of a multi-million dollar contract is a lot of bribe money. The gentleman sharing this information, however, does not allow the practice within his realm of authority.

Bribes are not harmless local practices. They cloud the judgment of the people who commit their companies to contracts for millions or even hundreds of millions of dollars.

Various government agents are so poorly paid in some countries that they are more or less expected to supplement their income with whatever they can extract off the record in the process of doing their jobs. Still, the idea of *negotiating* a bribe amount struck me as a contortion of an illegality.

The director of a South American moving company fully expanded the company into all the available work space. Needing more room, he built onto the existing building, knowing that he would have to pay off the government building inspector if he did so. It was considered in the cost of the new space. But then it was also a law that a company with more than fifty employees must provide a cafeteria and free lunch for them, and the director felt he had to have every square meter as productive space.

The inspector came around monthly for a little chat on how the building was in deviation of the code and there was no cafeteria for the employees. The director would agree, and a penalty fee would change hands without a receipt. It was not a small amount.

One month, the inspector made his visit but this time he insisted on an exorbitant amount. They discussed the situation, in effect negotiating the amount of the illegal bribe.

Finally, an amount was settled on, paid, and the inspector went away until the next month.

The director accepts the fact that he will be paying the monthly bribe as long as his company occupies that building. The option is to tear it down and build it legally.

Some deals just aren't what they purport to be. Take the beauty parlor deal in the capitol city of a very conservative Arabic country. A very wealthy Arabian prince (is there any other kind?) who was a regular customer of Western Capital Corp used his influence to get a start-up loan for a lady friend of his to open a beauty parlor. He didn't want to loan the money to her directly, but would guarantee the bank's loan. A good building was found and was nicely outfitted and staffed.

One fine day after the salon was in operation, the bank account manager, Mr. Yamamoto (of the first chapter) decided to visit his account. Since it was on the way to his house, he just dropped by unannounced at about 5:30 on a Wednesday afternoon. He figured that there would be a lot of activity as ladies got ready for the week-end, since this would correspond to Friday afternoon in the week pattern of the non-Muslim world.

What he found was five remarkably beautiful women, unveiled, lounging around in the salon doing each other's hair and nails. They did not run for their veils when he entered. There were no customers. Mr. Yamamoto was shown the premises. Upstairs were five little bedrooms, sparsely furnished.

Back downstairs, he asked, "Where are all the customers?" The beauty parlor had been showing a profit on the early reports, so there had to be customers.

The salon manager rather vaguely answered, "Oh, they usually come later in the evening."

The account manager pondered the source of the cash flow, known to bankers as the "first way out." He realized that it was the heavily made-up women doing their purple-red, dagger-like nails. He "called" the loan first thing the next business day, but the deal has ever since been known as "the whorehouse that WCC financed."

I told this story to a group of WCC officers at a business dinner on a Caribbean island nation. In that moment of silence after the laughter stopped, the senior officer of that country very softly said, "We did the same thing." His subordinates gasped, and waited in stunned silence for some kind of explanation.

"It's true," he continued. "It wasn't a beauty parlor, though. It was a small hotel, a very pretty one, in fact. Its purpose became obvious when the account officer went by for a routine checking and found only a series of small rooms with no furniture except a bed. There were no closets, no wardrobes, no dresser. Just a bed. Downstairs in the entry room were several lovely young women who definitely were not chambermaids. We got out of the loan as fast as we could."

There's an adage among bankers that may apply here: "Never loan money on a chicken farm." This is because if the loan went into default, the bank would have to possess the farm and all the chickens and manage a work-out process, which bankers would not want to be called upon to do. If the above beauty parlor or hotel had gone bust, who would have managed the work-out?

It is acceptable for business people to put this book on "Pause" while you go check on a few clients.

Doing business in other cultures is fascinating, challenging, frustrating, and often rewarding. The unexpected is routine, and the cross-cultural may be mystifying. But beware. Stimulation is addictive.

By Their Companies Ye Shall Know Them

A top level senior executive of one of the largest and richest financial institutions in the world sat, a number of years ago, in the office of the Minister of Finance of an African nation. He was on a mission to collect on some past due loans from the government of this nation, and, incidentally, to hunt large game. He fully expected to take back some trophies for his walls and some cash for his company.

I shall call him Mr. Richards, the lion-hearted, with apologies to the historical character.

Mr. Richards was expensively dressed, clean and well groomed in every detail except his tongue. Other senior officers of his company knew that he was given to the use of foul expletives and derogatory comments, but he would never talk that way in front of clients. Today, he was speaking through his translator.

The African was holding a firm position. Either he was a tough negotiator, or he didn't realize how much he had to lose by not cutting a deal with the American. Talking through a translator drags, and Mr. Richards became impatient. He chewed on his ever-present cigar and got looser and more insistent.

"Tell this mother-forsaken African..." etc. Or, "Who the hoot does he think he's talking to? Tell him I said,..." blah, blah, blah. The translator was having to clean up everything before relaying it. Mr. Richards should have realized that tone of voice does not need translation.

The African Minister was patient, making sure that each understood the position of the other.

At the end of the conference, Mr. Richards told his translator to close with the usual diplomatic crap. It was time to get out of there. So the translator said all the right words as they stood and stepped forward to shake hands and leave.

The African Minister also stood, shook hands, and said in perfect British-accented English, "Thank you for your time, sir. It has been a pleasure to become acquainted with you." For he was a graduate of Oxford University.

A senior executive visited Saudi Arabia, swinging wide to review the troops, so to speak, on the way to his annual big game hunt in Africa. Anne, the wife of the in-country senior, was expecting him for lunch at the executive housing, and the air conditioning had broken down. She had called the maintenance crew and went upstairs to get on some make-up.

When Anne came downstairs again, there was a middle-aged fellow dressed in khaki pants and a short-sleeved shirt standing in the middle of the living room, looking around. She didn't know that maintenance had shipped in a new employee, but she sailed right into an explanation of the air conditioner problem. He looked rather curious and didn't have much to contribute to the discussion.

The houseboy came into the room silently, bearing a tray with cool water and fresh dates. She suddenly realized that the houseboy would not do this for a maintenance man. He must have let in the president of her husband's corporation while she was upstairs. Anne had never even heard the doorbell. With adept word-work, she steered the conversation away from the air conditioner vents and the fuse box and bade him be seated in the living room.

Anne told this story on herself, and we all had a good laugh—after the visiting senior had left on the corporate plane.

Heaven knows, we wouldn't want the visiting corporate seniors to know what our life is really like out in the boonies. I remember one winter, relatively speaking, when a group of visiting seniors came with their wives on the corporate plane. In the winter in Saudi Arabia, flowers would bloom and the gardeners might even grow some tomatoes. Normally, I would wait until the temperature was below one hundred degrees Fahrenheit before I would play tennis, but in the winter we could play before 10 p.m.

A dinner was given for the guests in the senior compound, where chicken and hamburgers were grilled out in the garden by the pool. Various liquid refreshments were served at the cost of three hundred dollars a bottle—liquids which were not normally available for our company get-togethers. It was a lovely evening.

They flew back to America and cut our cost of living pay by five percent. Okay, so cost of living pay has nothing to do with hardship pay. It's just the principle of the thing.

Seniors are not always so unsympathetic, though. My beautiful jogging friend in Indonesia found the wife of the visiting company president fully understanding of the conditions under which she ran every day.

"How can you jog in this filthy air thick with exhaust fumes? Aren't you afraid to run at the edge of the road in such dangerous traffic? I don't know how you can bear to live in a city like this," she said.

And the lovely jogger listened silently, because everything she thought of saying was censored, like, "Well, your husband sent us here, lady."

Visiting seniors are a fact of ex-pat life. One hopes they will be well-briefed and sensitive to the local business and social environment. If not, however, their visits make great gossip fodder.

Getting the Job

An attractive young woman was called back for further interviews concerning an overseas executive position with an international home appliance firm. In the final round, she had lunch with the Latin American director at a fine restaurant. Things were going well until she swallowed a hunk of meat prematurely and literally began to choke to death.

The senior executive, well trained in problem recognition, swiftly came to her aid by administering the Heimlich maneuver. The meat was dislodged and her life was saved.

With remarkable *savoir faire*, she was able to continue the lunch and the interview. She got the job.

Interviewing is, at best, an imperfect method to size up a potential employee. Once a short list of candidates has been selected from written applications and references, though, the personal presentation is the next step. Some unusual things come out in interviews.

Young Japanese applicants were known to be very frank on the subject of sex long before sex was so frankly discussed by others. Some fifteen years ago, a middle-aged American personnel officer, a single woman, asked the routine question of a young man, "Do you have any children?"

His answer was much more complete than required: he and his wife felt that they regretably could not yet afford children, but meanwhile they were having intercourse a certain number of times per week, and were using such-and-such birth control.

The interviewer waited out the answer and looked for a less personal question to ask.

David, a corporate officer, was asked be one of three people giving interviews to entry-level candidates, which was not usually part of his job. It was an interesting experience. One of the candidates particularly sticks in David's mind.

The exceedingly well dressed, somewhat arrogant young man entered the small interviewing room where David was seated behind a small desk. The applicant asked if he might be allowed to make himself more comfortable by removing his suit jacket, and was of course given permission. He made a show of taking off the jacket and draping it over the back of his chair, turning the lapel back so that the brand name "Armani" was revealed. He wore fashionable wide red suspenders, and David also noted that his silk tie was by Hermes. And then the applicant did a most unusual thing: he crossed one leg at a right angle over the other and pulled up the trouser quite a bit away from the ankle. David thought that this was probably in order to point out that he wore over-the-calf black socks favored by professionals. The applicant had graduated from the right schools and had all the answers, but he didn't get the job.

Mr. Peterson was a senior executive at a consulting firm when he was asked to interview young Mr. Frist. Being a second round interview, Mr. Peterson invited Mr. Frist to lunch. Beginning light chatter as they entered the restaurant, Mr. Frist asked, "Where did you go to graduate school, sir?"

"Tuck School of Business. How do you feel about your M.B.A. from Harvard?" he asked in return.

Mr. Frist's reply was so exuberant that, he declared, he could not imagine why anyone would ever want to go to any other business school. Having just determined that his interviewer had in fact done so, this was not the best possible response.

Seated and studying the menus, the young man thanked Mr. Peterson for the opportunity to have a personal interview. "I do so poorly on paper," he said. "I always have trouble expressing myself in written form. There is nothing I hate worse than filling out forms and writing reports. Just give me a chance to talk person-to-person. That's how I can best present myself."

Since he was applying for a consulting job which is primarily executed on paper, in carefully written reports, Mr. Peterson was not in agreement with the interviewee's self-assessment. They finished the lunch, shook hands cordially, and never saw each other again.

And then there was the American job applicant who wrote to a General Motors executive in Australia. His letter opened, "I am so sorry that I am not able to write to you in your native language."

A credit analyst for a major credit card company in the Far East was interested in making a career shift into an international financial institution. After the usual beginning questions, the interviewing officer asked her to define her current job and discuss her responsibilities. She got into the subject with enthusiasm, speaking highly of the credit card company and its services even though she planned to leave it. She even recommended that the interviewer get one of the cards, and offered to process his application before resigning. Her cheerfulness, vigor, loyalty, and pleasant relationship with her employer came though well. The interviewer didn't need another credit card, but he gave her the credit analysis job for which she was applying.

Sometimes the system works.

Getting Good Help Nowadays

Once upon a time, in a land far away to the south where the people eat enormous portions of beef and say "si" when they mean "yes," a lady noticed that the walls of her home needed cleaning. She had a very good maid who was responsive to her every request, so she attempted to tell the maid to mix soap with water and wash the walls with it. The maid got very busy, and the lady left to do some errands. The lady spoke Spanish well, but was not a native Spanish speaker. She made a mistake in giving the directions: she had told the maid to mix *sopa* and water, but *sopa* is soup, not soap. So the maid dutifully mixed up some bouillon cubes with hot water and tried to wash the walls with the yellowish beef-flavored solution. It did not get the walls clean.

Could it be that our maids think we are all crazy foreigners who have never worked and don't know anything about housekeeping anyway? Or maybe it is because we pay them several times what they would be paid by their own countrywomen and treat them like human beings as well. They are so anxious to keep their jobs that they would do anything—no matter how ridiculous—to keep us happy. Some of the flub-ups are language problems, as the case above, but not all.

The same lady with the soup-glazed walls was married to a man from Chile, so his native language was Spanish. She woke up rather ill one morning, and her husband insisted that she stay in bed and he would get the children off to school. On the way out, he spoke to the maid in Spanish, telling her to prepare a tray and take it up to the señora, who was sick in bed. He instructed the maid to put a bowl, cereal, milk, orange juice and coffee on the tray. And she did exactly that: she took the lady a tray bearing a bowl filled with cereal, milk, orange juice, and coffee, all mixed together.

Well, we don't hire these people to be rocket scientists. A willing spirit is the finest quality of a good maid. I certainly have a wonderful person waxing my floors even as I write this. Her name is Gina, and she is a dear. When the basics are done, she looks for work to do. She stacks tee-shirts and underwear in perfect rows on our closet shelves. She stands everything at attention even if it has to be leaned against the wall, such as tubes of toothpaste with only one squeeze left. She lines up shoes in pairs and cleans up our tennis shoes without being asked. What a gift! So I readily forgive her when she organizes everything in the food pantry by size or bottle shape when I have it organized by the type of food it is. We're working on that.

One morning I was dashing out to a meeting when I rushed past the television/guest room where we keep acres of books. *Whoa! Back up!* Gina was in the room with books everywhere, dusting, sorting and stacking them around the small room. Carefully, I asked what she was doing. She replied that she was cleaning and organizing the books.

"How are you organizing them?" I asked.

"By size," she cheerfully answered.

"But I have them organized by subject," I replied. Her face went absolutely white with shock, because she had no idea what those books were about, and had no way of finding out. Later, I spent a couple of hours re-sorting them.

She does clean relentlessly. Silverplated decorative objects are now down to their less decorative base metal. The silverplated tray needed replating anyway after all these years. She only made the need more urgent. The gold-coated throats of my cloisonné vases are reduced to gleaming copper. I never thought to tell her that gold does not need to be polished with Brasso. How can you fault a person for doing a job too well?

There are many things that we have known for most of our lives that are New and Different to the household helpers we hire overseas. How about the maid who never learned how to open the door to get out of a car? Or the Panamanian houseboy who was told to turn out all the lights downstairs when the American couple went up to bed? Apprehensively, he traced each light cord until he found where it went into the wall. Standing back, he gave a sharp tug. Sure enough, the plug was jerked out of the socket, and the light turned off. Will wonders never cease?

When we lived in Saudi Arabia, most of the maids were from Somalia. I tried out one potential maid—briefly—who did not know how to turn on a wall light switch and was afraid to plug in the vacuum. She thought that the bedspread went directly on top of the bare mattress and one sheet went over the bedspread. While I was willing to train a maid, I wanted to start at a little higher level.

The next applicant had a lot more going for her, but I did not qualify by her standards. The first day she found the bread I was letting mold in the kitchen, which was to be used for my biology class at the international school in Riyadh. I prevented her from throwing it away without being able to adequately explain why. My Arabic was rudimentary at best, and she was from Somalia anyway. Arabic was not her native language.

The second day she found two apples that I was drying in a window to make those funny-faced dolls, and again I wouldn't let her throw them away.

The third day I brought home a well and truly dissected large white rat for my young son to examine, since the biology class was finished with the lab. I put it on top of the desk in his room for him to find when he came in from sports. She found it first. She left and never came back.

We set ourselves up for disappointment when we expect an employee to read our minds and do things just as we want them done, assuming that he or she would know how that is. Helen, the wife of an American embassy official in an African country, tells of the time she hired a waiter to assist her in giving an embassy dinner. This fellow was supposed to be the most wonderful waiter and general dinner assistant in the city.

At the market that day she had bought some langoustas, those delicious miniature lobsters, to serve as appetizers. The waiter arrived at about four o'clock and started to boil them. She wanted them to be boiled at the last minute for a better flavor, so she stopped him.

At about eight that night, he was serving the precious tidbits, shelled, laid out on a lovely dish and covered with a red sauce of his own fabrication. Helen noticed that everyone took one but never accepted a second. She was busy and rather nervous to be giving her first embassy dinner in that country for a lot of important guests. She didn't check out the langousta hors d'oeuvres until all the guests were gone. Finally tasting the tender tidbits, she was stunned to find that the langoustas had been served shelled and sauced but totally raw.

Sometimes an employee is hired that is supposed to be just the greatest and best ever, but the person doesn't fit with the employer's expectations. There was an embassy family in the Congo that had never been able to hire a satisfactory cook, and they desperately needed one for the constant embassy dinners. A Pakistani family had moved their own Spanish cook to the Congo with them, and they were about to move again. The cook did not want to make the next move with them. So the Spanish cook agreed to live with and work for my friends.

In the weeks before the transfer, my friend was constantly praising the wonderful new Spanish cook to her staff, saying how marvelous everything was going to be when the cook finally came. She was indeed an excellent cook, but she turned out to be a slovenly woman who instantly trained the rest of the servants to cater to her whims. When she trimmed lettuce in the kitchen, the trimmings were dropped to the floor for others to clean up. When she returned from the market, she had one of the other servants clean her shoes while she stood royally in them.

My friend soon began to plot how to get rid of the cook she had so recently coveted. She was very fortunate when the family of the military attaché moved to town and wanted to hire her. Finally, my friend was able to return to her cook-less but harmonious status.

It hardly seemed fair that this same gracious lady had so much trouble with squabbling among the servants during their embassy duty in Yugoslavia. She came in from shopping one day to find two of the men fighting with knives under the dining room table.

But normally, cooks and maids are such a blessing in overseas life. Of course, cleaning is harder without the homes, machines, and modern materials that we have available in the developed world. With this advantage, however, families often make servants a necessity by leasing too large a house. Ex-pats often choose the largest and most complicated house possible with the allowance provided by the employer.

Moreover, servants often would rather make very little money but work in families or groups. First thing you know, you are running a cross between kindergarten and soap opera.

A potential renter was being shown through a large house in Rio de Janeiro. The current resident, a Brazilian woman, was giving the three-floor tour. It was obvious that the house received a lot of care from many servants—far more than ex-pats would ever hire. Employment had snowballed when the resident was begged to hire the sister of the cook, the daughter of the maid, and the wife of the guard.

The rental tour arrived in the attic, which was bare, but there was one room with a door to which tracks in the dust led. The potential renter opened the door and found a large closet with a bare light bulb hanging from the ceiling, one simple chair, and one overloaded ashtray.

"What is this room for?" she asked the resident.

"This is where I come to hide from my fourteen servants."

Even When We Try to Be Good

Charity is a major business. It becomes rapidly apparent when trying to administer charity funds in a developing country that all the arts of administration, communication, bookkeeping, and field reporting are necessary for effective use of funds and full accountability to the donors. The fact that we do this as volunteers must not affect our professionalism. We can't just put on our "goody two shoes" and sashay out into the poor, teeming masses handing out rupiah and rice with condescending smiles.

First, we devise and execute schemes to earn the money. Then we have committee meetings, write letters, and receive requests for projects. After determining which projects will receive grants, we must follow up to ensure that the money has been appropriately used. A well-run charity will usually become a continuing relationship with the donor group.

No doubt many will ask, "Why don't you ladies just go get a job?" It is because in these countries we are usually not allowed to have a work visa, unless we get an exception to work in health or education. The poorer countries must keep the jobs available for their own citizens.

Ex-pat wives often get involved personally in bathing orphan babies, teaching Braille or English, or advising income-generating projects and marketing their product. We get to know both foreigners and nationals who give their lives in selfless service. It is a fine privilege to participate directly in arranging cataract surgery for elderly poor people, or in job training for multiple-handicapped people and

71

lepers. We are profoundly aware of the wealth, education, and freedom we possess.

Thus robed in the air of professionalism and launched by the highest motives, the volunteer leaves the safety of the American Club and all-day bridge parties and deliberately throws herself into very foreign and possibly vulnerable positions.

A classic example of this is the annual trip of representatives of the Social Welfare Committee of the American Women's Association in Jakarta, Indonesia. We traveled at personal expense to places well off the tourist route to check on the projects which are—or might in the future be—funded by AWA.

Early one morning seven of us flew from Jakarta, taking successively smaller and rougher airplanes until we arrived in the hot, dusty, crowded and polluted city of Ujung Padang. We visited a leper colony and hospital in Ujung Padang, and spent the night in a very disappointing hotel whose name was remarkably similar to a fine hotel on the other side of town. From there we flew to Kendari on the east coast of the Indonesian island of Sulawesi.

For this last flight, a careful flight weight was needed for the small propeller plane. Each lady was required to stand on an industrial size platform scale bearing all her carry-on luggage and her purse. The foot-long needle above the scale swung up, up, and waggled on her fully loaded weight, shown not only to the whole committee but to the entire terminal audience. (This might be the solution to the over-booking problem back home, but I can't see it working in the Atlanta Hartsfield Airport.)

In Kendari, we were joined by an American doctor and his family who would escort us to some of the Save the Children projects with which he worked.

The doctor had set up an invitation to tea with the wife of the governor of the Kendari province, since it was politically necessary to do so. Our ranking committee member on this trip was a dedicated volunteer who nevertheless spoke

Passenger Weigh-in

very little Bahasa Indonesia. She had memorized a little self-introductory statement, which was, "Good morning, my name is Betty. I am the leader," and a few other pleasantries. The greeting was often met with confusion or an awkward silence, however, and Betty had no more words in her repertoire.

It was after tea at the governor's house that Ellie, the only committee member who was truly fluent in the Indonesian language, called Betty aside and asked what word she was using for "leader." "KECHua," she replied. "Isn't that right?"

Ever the mistress of tact, Ellie suggested that "keTUa" would be better. Betty had been introducing herself, in fact, as the "cockroach."

The adventure had not yet begun. Expecting to travel from Kendari in the air conditioned cabins of a nice cruiser, we learned after it was too late to back out that our reservations were regrettably not firm—that is, our agent had not paid as high a bribe as someone else. We traveled for sixteen hours, instead, on the coastal ferry which carried humans like cattle—and also cattle, indeed! We were at least in "staterooms," but they were closet-sized rooms each with four bunk beds and a tiny fan churning the hot, humid air. Below our deck was a large wood slat platform stretched over the bottom V of the ship where passengers not able to buy a "stateroom" sat, lay, played cards, nursed babies, and whatever else humans do in sixteen hours.

These passengers and gawkers who hopped aboard the boat at its stops were so overwhelmed by our presence that they watched us through the tiny stateroom window and clogged the walkway past the door, blocking any chance of a breeze. When we came onto the deck they stared into our faces from three inches away, touched us, and a few tried to talk to us in random bits of English.

When the boat chugged up to the port of the village of Raha during the night, men and boys swung like monkeys from other boats onto the deck of our ferry to sell bananas, candies, drinks, and rice concoctions wrapped in banana leaves. The word spread instantly through the town that white women were on the boat, and the landing was a mob scene of curious villagers, mostly men and boys, until the boat left about four hours later. Since we were traveling without our husbands and children, most of the men assumed that we were not nice ladies.

Some of our committee never came out of their closets and never went to the bathroom for the entire sixteen hours. Others chose to go into Raha in shifts, leaving a guard in the stateroom at all times.

The second shift of hungry ladies had just gotten their bowls of rice and chicken bones in a little restaurant when young men ran in excitedly and by means of a few words and many gestures made them understand that the boat was leaving them. They paid without eating, ran back to the dock, and seethed in hunger and the awful heat for two more hours at the dock and about eight more hours of the trip.

The destination was Baubau on the island of Buton. How much more primitive could it get? Actually, the village of Baubau and the lovely people we met in making our calls were such a relief. The *losman* where we stayed was not, but hey, two out of three ain't bad. What's a *losman*? Well, you know what a hotel is? Now, do you know what a hostel is? Back up about two more steps, and you've got a *losman*.

One of our members arrived weak and proceeded to be profoundly sick. She stayed in bed, to use the term loosely, the entire time we were in Baubau. She was cared for by a friend and checked frequently by the doctor, but she was miserable indeed.

The next morning we packed with the good doctor, his family, and drivers into two black vans (Why do they have black vehicles in the tropics?) and bounced off down the paved road to the gravel road to the dirt trail to the public health center which served the colony of families transplanted from the island of Bali. These gracious people came for the baby weigh-in, inoculations, and demonstrations about nutrition.

After we arrived, they made it known that they had prepared lunch for us. There was an impromptu performance of Balinese music and dance, and then we piled back into the black vans to a nearby health center which had chairs set up for us on the front porch around a big table.

The hosts served us warm 7-Up with much bowing and welcoming, but the tepid, sweet drink hardly helped our raging thirst. With much fanfare, a man bore on his shoulder an enormous *yanka* (jackfruit), which is a local delight but something of an acquired taste. Jackfruit has a certain sweet, cloying mustiness.

To my left, Joanne groaned. She knew jackfruit well from her years in Brazil, and she hated it. Now jackfruit has never been one of my favorite foods, but I can eat it in a pinch. Joanne and I worked out a system whereby she would take the fruit in her right hand, eventually drop her hand by her side and pass it to me. Dozens of people on the porch and in the yard pushed close to watch the honored guests eat the fruit. Pretending to be delighted, I ate mine and hers. The plate came around again. I ate mine and put hers in my purse. Then TAA-DAA!! the HEART of the jackfruit! The very best part! I was a little full of jackfruit, but this was an honor we had to accept.

We smiled a lot, shook a lot of hands, bragged about babies and took pictures. Then the doctor whispered those awful words: "I'm not sure, but from what I think I'm hearing, well, I don't think this was 'lunch.' "

It wasn't. Back into the black vans, down a dirt road we went, burping jackfruit as we bounced to the humble home of the local doctor where many ladies had worked all day to put together the finest of the best that they could offer. This was a command performance, folks. As the guide pointed out, they couldn't afford this, and they were treating us like queens. So we ate chicken curry and pork something and vegetables and the ever-present rice. There were even two desserts.

Now as it happened, the lady who managed the *losman* was still in a huff because we hadn't eaten her food the night before. We didn't know that she was assuming we would eat our evening meals in her dining room when we came to sleep there. Earlier that day she had literally gotten it in writing that we were having lunch that day at her *losman*. Well, a very few made it to the table back at the *losman* a couple of hours later, but we all paid for the meal. The leftovers from that lunch were served at every meal thereafter until we packed out.

There was a lot of beautiful hill country along the island coast, and we were told of a particular waterfall that we should see. Through Ellie, we talked with the three drivers about going to the somewhat remote area.

"Do you know about this lovely waterfall?" she asked.

"Yes, of course we know it."

"Do you know exactly where it is?"

"Yes, everyone knows where it is."

"Could you take us to it?"

"Yes, we can drive you part of the way and then you would walk the last half mile or so." And it was inserted into the plan for the afternoon.

But first we would accept the invitation to tea at the *kraton* (palace) of the aging former prince of Baton. The kraton was an enormous house overlooking the blue sea. It was hardly our idea of a palace, though. The floor was constructed of rough wood planks through which we could see the ground, and the roof was corrugated, galvanized metal. After the grand tour and history lesson, we were served hot sweet tea and—surprise!—Dunkin' Donuts which had come by boat from the big city only a week before. Such an honor!

About that waterfall: it was getting late, and not everyone wanted to drive to the nearest access road and then hike to the falls. We were trying to come to some agreement among ourselves when Ellie overheard the drivers discussing our crazy plans. "Why do they want to see it?" they asked. "It's dry this time of year." Ellie then inquired very directly about the current state of the waterfall, and the trip was dropped. Once again we learned that you have to ask the right questions.

The charity trip being finished, and our most desperately ill member being well enough to travel, we returned to Ujung Padang and again spent the night there. But this time, we located the nice hotel where we were supposed to stay instead of the dump with a similar name in which we stayed on the way over. We were overwhelmed by its beautiful restaurant with clean, white tablecloths and air conditioning. Wonderful foods were listed on the menu. As Joanne wrote in her memoirs, "If it was flambé, we ordered it." Ahhh, civilization.

That trip resulted in our granting, or continuing to grant, funds to a leprosy hospital, health clinic, infant feeding and nutritional education programs, and to the funding of a well for a leper colony which had no water source within two miles.

There were a number of projects over the years which did not get funds approved. You be the judge of the following requests:

➢A very poor village requested that the American Women's Association finance a food-generating project of raising chickens. The sum would cover cages, enough grain to start, and five hundred male chicks. We declined, feeling that it would be difficult to make the chicken hatchery self-perpetuating if all the chicks were male. We strongly suspected that the chicks might be diverted into the illegal cock fights which were very popular gambling events.

➢A group of blind masseuses were struggling to maintain their honorable living when other women—who were not even blind—took away their clientele and massaged more than tired muscles. They therefore petitioned us to give them one room in the AWA office where they could massage women. Free massages to the AWA Board and the Social Welfare Committee were proposed in place of paying rent. We rejected this idea for several reasons, truthfully telling them that we couldn't possibly spare a room.

➤In South America, the International Newcomer's Club, a large organization of English-speaking women from all nations, is engaged in a certain amount of charity work. For several months they had been helping to support an orphanage. The Board of Directors decided that more lasting good would result if the orphanage had an income-generating activity, and this would prevent the home from being dependent upon foreign charity.

The dear grandmother and her daughter who ran the orphanage agreed, and they accepted a hot dog cart, everything needed to prepare hot dogs, and the initial stock of foods. The older orphans would push the cart through the neighborhood after school, making enough money to buy good food for the babies, too.

The plan had been in operation for several weeks when the charity chairperson dropped by the orphanage unannounced and got quite a shock. There was no orphanage. There were no orphans. The building housed a factory, and the grandmother and her daughter were lazing around outside—eating hot dogs.

The whole orphanage was a scam from the first day. They simply moved the factory out and rounded up neighborhood kids when the charity committee person was expected. Thereafter, unannounced visits became standard procedure for all charity relationships.

➤When a request was made for funds by what seemed to be a worthy group, the charity committee sent some information and asked them to return the enclosed form as soon as possible. And they did return it quickly, practically by return mail. It had not been filled out, but it was returned as soon as possible, just as had been requested. You just can't assume anything.

➤There was one plan we were asked to support in Asia which would have started up a small onion farm on some unused land adjacent to an orphanage. The orphan boys would do all the work, learn something about farming, and help raise both their own onions and some money for the home. The charity group initially agreed to the grant, and then learned that the orphanage meant to receive the $1,500 not for the start-up, not even for the whole first year, but every month for at least eighteen months. Considering that onions grow several crops a year in the tropics and there should be no need to keep buying new seed onions, we decided that the project stank.

In Jakarta, there is one central committee, BKKKS,[1] which attempts to co-ordinate the activities of some twenty-five charity committees of all countries. The free exchange of information helps us to distribute our time and contributions more wisely, and, frankly, keeps us from getting rooked. These people know more than we can hope to learn about Indonesian charity.

At one of these meetings, Betty, our leader on the Sulawesi trip, was explaining our justification for large and continuing support for a certain orphanage in Bali. Bali is a Hindu island, she explained, and Hindu people don't support charities, believing that suffering in this life gains merit for future lives. They don't have charity for their own people, she elaborated, so outside groups have to help them.

One of the BKKKS members had locked Betty's eyes with her own, and Betty noticed for the first time the bright "tika" on her forehead which married Hindu women wear. The more Betty tried to talk her way out of what was coming through as a religious put-down and an ethnic insult, the deeper she sank. She swore later that the tika on the woman's forehead grew larger and larger and began to pulse into Betty's eyes as a severe expression burned on her face.

---

[1]   You will never need to know the lengthy Indonesian words for which BKKKS stands. Trust me.

Unable to extract herself, Betty finally sputtered out and mumbled to a close.

Being politically correct in such a mixed group is incredibly difficult. It is only our sense of mercy that unites us. The Hindu lady was also merciful that day, and never reminded Betty in any way of her gaffe.

So we may look a little foolish, even when we try to do good. We are deceived sometimes. It's a small price to pay to get deeply involved in the foster land, and meet those citizens who work tirelessly to improve the health and living conditions of their own people. They are the heroines long after ex-pat volunteers have returned home or have been transferred to yet another country.

The beauty of our volunteerism is that it helps us cope with the moral pressure of living in poor countries as if we were rich—for we are by comparison. It is more than a sense of *noblesse oblige*, more than a justification of having what others have not. It is a proving ground to determine if our philosophies of religion and life are valid.

Women at Work

Betty and Jennifer were having dinner with other single working women in a cozy Italian restaurant in São Paulo. Jennifer was openly angry about how her job had turned out. A young bonds trader, she was rising rapidly in her corporation in Chicago when a Brazilian client, a man of great personal wealth distributed in several companies, offered her a job. She initially declined, but he countered over the following weeks with a very high salary, a sign-on bonus, and her dream job description. He even paid for her flight down, during which time she spent the week-end with his wife and family in the country. She was thrilled with all the attention and professional promises, and finally resigned from her job in Chicago and moved to Brazil.

Jennifer was to be head of the bonds trading office, so she came in with plans and ideas learned in her American master's degree and practiced in the prior agency. Although there was a lot of hoopla over her arrival, she soon found her operating plan and her management attempts to be undercut and thwarted at every turn. Her instructions were finally blatantly disregarded, and she was often told, "Go check with the boss." And every confrontation with him became more heated.

Show-down day came at last. She stormed into the owner's office over the latest incident. He was missing opportunities, he was losing money, while all her obviously-better-American-way plan was going down the tubes. Why had he spent so much money to bring her down here if he wasn't going to allow her to do the job?

The boss quit yelling and swearing at Jennifer long enough to swivel his chair to face her with an unnatural calm. "I hired an American woman with an excellent degree and work experience because I thought it would give my agency a lot of prestige in Brazil. That's all I want from you—just that my clients know that you are here."

Jennifer immediately began to plan to not be there.

If the boss had gotten her residence visa and work permit as he had promised, Jennifer might have had a bit more time to find another job and stay in Brazil, which would have pleased her. As it was, she was already not exactly legally in Brazil. On the day she left her job, she wouldn't have any cover to remain there at all.

Betty took over the conversation while Jennifer gave attention back to her cooling pasta.

Without naming her employer, she said that she had been hired from the United States to work as an executive in a fairly small office. In the same office with her was a man who was at her same level in the organizational chart.

There was one telephone in the room. When it rang, the other executive frequently asked her to answer it, feigning concentration on something at hand. He was never rude, but this practice usurped her time, and she found a way to bring up the subject eventually.

"It's really quite simple," he answered, "and I hope you don't mind. But I would like for you to always answer the phone so that when my clients call, they think I have a secretary." She minded. They worked out a more equitable arrangement.

I still have not met a woman working overseas who says she would rather have stayed home. But they agree, to a person, that the gains for women's rights in the workplace have not filtered down to South America.

It's for You

In Saudi Arabia, however, it is still illegal for women to work except in health and education. A few years ago, a married executive couple was hired to work for a certain American corporation. Every work day a car with curtains over the passenger windows—not that unusual in Saudi—picked her up inside her compound walls and drove her to work. The car entered the underground garage of the company and dislodged her into the elevator. She went upstairs to an office which had no public access, and did her job within the walls of the corporation.

There were a few female secretaries during that time, who were the trailing spouses of men employed in the Kingdom. When the local authorities came to ensure that females were not being employed, a signal was sounded and they went to a certain place where a black, curtained van was always waiting to take them home. They were never arrested during those years, which is good for their husbands. Had they been caught, their husbands would have been jailed for not properly controlling their "personal property."

We've come a long way, baby.

There are certainly a lot of countries outside the Developed World in which women, both local hires and ex-pats, routinely work as respected executives, secretaries, and professionals. Sometimes countries make this change over a period of economic crisis, when women must join the work force in order to support the family. Having made the break, then, the possibility is opened for others. The struggle isn't over, though, until they receive equal pay for equal work.

A lovely young female executive was sent to Tokyo in her new position with one of the most prominent soft drink firms. To her dismay, she discovered that the national-hire male executives considered her to be "available," as she delicately put it. She carefully guarded her body language and every expression while they caught on to the fact that she was to be considered a business professional, regardless of gender.

The concept of offering meaningful employment to the trailing spouse of the primary employee has finally begun to come into its own. It makes a lot of sense, considering the cost of supporting an executive abroad, to get two for the price of one move.

About seventeen years ago, however, a group of executive trainees was about to receive assignments in the Middle East. They and their spouses were invited to the stunning home of the area director, which was situated on a mountainside overlooking Athens, Greece. We were a bit nervous about this "parading of the beef."

The area director, Mr. Hite, visited each little cluster to make himself available for questions. Most had none, or found themselves strangely tongue-tied. Lara, however, asked if it would be possible for wives to find work in the Middle East.

"What is your degree in?" asked Mr. Hite.

"I have a Ph.D. in language acquisition," she answered. Lara was modest. We knew that, as a Peace Corps volunteer, she had been the first person ever to record a certain African language in a form which was used by its own tribe.

"Do you type?" countered Mr. Hite.

"No," answered Lara somewhat tentatively, perhaps meaning that she would not type for a living.

"Why don't you learn something useful?" suggested Mr. Hite.

About the least politically correct suggestion that could be made at this juncture would be Mr. Hite's other comment, "Why don't you 'just' stay home and have children?" And yet I recently received a call from a woman to thank me for encouraging her family to move abroad. This entailed the wife's putting on hold her stellar career as a Certified Public Accountant (CPA) for a renown tax firm. She was already at the management level and rising fast.

Giving precedence to her husband's career, she moved overseas and volunteered as a parental teacher assistant in one child's class, became very involved in her younger son's speech therapy, perfected a fourth major language, and then seriously took up oil painting for which she has tremendous talent. Most importantly, she established a new relationship with her young children and derived great pleasure from being home with them.

She said that she would never have had these experiences if she had stayed where she could have continued as a CPA. She was glad she had made the move. And she will probably go back to her career as soon as possible, with the family on much better footing.

For women who want to work overseas, careful advisement is essential for a successful experience. Always remember, the Bill of Rights and the Equal Rights Amendment are American,[2] and they do not cross borders with you. What was fought for on home soil was not necessarily won elsewhere.

---

[2]   Other nationalities will please substitute appropriate equivalents.

The Trailing Spouse

The golf starter on an Asian island put together an impromptu foursome. The players introduced themselves and shook hands.

"What brings you to this country?" the American executive asked the tall, handsome Indian.

"The ambassador of {a major western country}," he answered. He was, in fact, her trailing significant other.

A bit later the American inquired, "What business interests to you have?"

"I dabble in horses and real estate," he replied. He obviously enjoyed his status. And so the age-old relationships switch places and keep marching.

Recent estimates from several sources agree that about twelve per cent of employees moved overseas are women. Some are the "primary hire," and others are considered the "trailing spouse" or "accompanying spouse" who is searching for meaningful employment at the same time. "Trailing spouse" is a neat piece of jargon. When I started following my husband from country to country, I was a Multinational Corporate Wife, or MNC Wife. The response is, of course, "But I'm not married to the corporation."

Trailing spouse is just as likely to refer to a husband following his wife's employment overseas. Then it is the man who is fighting the red tape battle because she has a work permit and he doesn't. He may have to go through a time of being an unemployed house husband. (Response: "But I'm not married to a house.") Life can proceed as usual, though. He learns to discuss electrical problems with workmen who mumble in strange accents that the language school never taught him. She learns to read contracts and credit reports and hopes she hasn't just agreed to give away the shop. Or the husband copes with hyperinflation at the grocery store and his wife discovers that even 30% *per month* return on investment may yield a net loss of 12%.[3]

Research on a country-by-country basis must be done to determine whether the accompanying spouse is legally able to continue to work as an executive or professional, or will be bureaucratically limited to work in health and education. There may also be positions available in embassies and consulates. These are few, however, since embassy or consulate jobs are offered first to their own trailing spouses.

Then one considers the create-a-job possibilities: freelance writing and photography, catering, consulting within a professional field, family counseling, or work linked by modem and express delivery from the home to its market anywhere in the world. Freelance accounting on the home computer is another idea. After a few years in the new area, and with the right skills and personality, one could work with an international resettling service. More places to look for employment are with the American Chamber of Commerce and other national commerce groups, international culture affiliations, or in the ubiquitous language schools.

If the trailing spouse is seriously considered for a job out of the home, the employer may be able to arrange for a work permit. It helps if the prospective employer can convincingly argue that the job has peculiar requirements for which this applicant is best suited. That is, the position could not adequately be filled by a local citizen. Obviously, taking an employment opportunity from a citizen and giving it to an ex-pat is a no-no. Therefore, the job description may require an applicant, for example, who speaks English and Swahili, has experience negotiating in Russia, and whose eyes are green on alternate Tuesdays. Surely the only

---

[3]   Brazil, June 1994

applicant who fits the designer description is the one the employer wanted to hire anyway.

Occasionally, there is an unexpected advantage in the job search for an ex-pat spouse. Consider the British publishing houses that give priority to secretarial applicants with American accents. Passing over excellent British applicants, the publishers often hire an American for the international prestige derived from having the phone answered with that accent. The opposite might be true on the other side of the pond. There are lots of possibilities.

One of the unexpected benefits of women's liberation is the way it has liberated men. A professional couple transferred to South America decided that the wife would take a few years to have a baby and stay at home until the child went to school. Then the husband was sent to a very good position in Europe, and the family established their home there. Within a year or so, he was disillusioned with the job and felt trapped while the wife was just itching to get back into the fray. In his last correspondence, he was seriously considering being a full-time father and offering his wife a turn as the financial supporter of the family. It doesn't really matter to our discussion if that happens or not. The important thing is that he is free to do that.

Part of the beauty of being a trailing spouse is that we not only re-introduce ourselves every few years; we can re-*define* ourselves. We uproot home and family to transplant them at the requirements of the "primary hire". Somewhere over the ocean we may decide that we were too involved in the last country with certain activities that lost their meaning, or which our families outgrew. It's time for a change. So we can start off in the next country not by saying, "I used to be a teacher," but perhaps with, "I play the stock market on my home computer," or "I'm writing my first historical romance novel." Make it up yourself. Figure out how to do it in the new setting and become whoever you wish to be.

The modern evolution of the seven year itch comes to light.

Fingernail Marks on the Armrest

Sally was a timid person who moved to Buenos Aires with her husband. Instead of buying a car, they used the services of a *remise*, a driver with his own car who works by the hour, the trip, the day, or whatever you need. Sally often reserved her favorite *remise* in advance. By Argentine standards, he was a fairly safe driver. Sally spoke very little Spanish, and the driver rarely spoke at all. They had a good working relationship.

Then came the day when Sally was running a little late. As she got into the car, she said only two words, "Please hurry." She thought they would be the last words she ever spoke. He drove on his side of the road for a while, and then on the opposing side. He ran red lights and jumped green lights. She was trembling so badly when she arrived that she could hardly walk. Lesson learned.

Training and licensing drivers is a terrible bother and a national expense, but an idea that many fairly modern countries need to institute. Can you imagine a major country that gives licenses to its drivers without any kind of test whatsoever, either written or driven? Many countries do. Others slide over the paperwork drill, collect a fee, and set people on the road who can not see nor do they know how to drive. What's more, they are hired by ex-pats who have been trained to drive carefully and courteously. There are fingernail marks on the armrests to prove it.

A few years ago, our son was on a trip to Bangkok with his school swim team to compete with four other international school teams. It's a wonderful opportunity to make friends in the international circuit and have lots of clean fun.

As in many Asian cities, a popular and inexpensive form of taxi is a motor scooter fitted with a rear cab, called a "took-took" in Bangkok. The cab fits two or maybe three small passengers. One evening, the team was told to get themselves from the school to the place where the final awards dinner would be held. Eight athletes were able to flag down two took-tooks. All the boys climbed in or on, and they took off laughing. Our son stood on the back bumper and held on to the little awning that covered the cab. The drivers were caught up in the spirit and didn't complain at the strain on their motors.

But these were highly competitive athletes, right? One of them leaned forward and said to the driver, "Five bahts extra if we beat the other took-took."

Five bahts were worth maybe twenty-five cents. The driver gunned the motor and pushed it as fast as it would go. The other driver and his passengers immediately rose to the competition. They wove between cars. They drove up on the sidewalk. They squeezed every second out of a stoplight. Taking an arched bridge over one of Bangkok's canals, they went airborne at the top and hit back down on the bridge at full tilt, nearly throwing Quinn over the side. They could have all died for a twenty-five cent victory. The challengers won the race, and all took the real prize—life for another day. They didn't race home.

In many cultures, being first in traffic is manhood, virility, power. It is one's self concept of the moment. In Venezuela, the one who loses out in traffic is a fool, a *bobo*. The winner is the *vivo*, the real man. The concept extends to any situation in which advantage can be taken, but is best illustrated in a car.

Being a *vivo* and making any potential rival look like a *bobo* is very important. Great risks may be taken to establish

The 5 Baht Race

who is superior between two strangers in any driving or parking situation.

Recently, a gentleman was cruising through a parking lot looking for a space. *Ah, there's one,* he thought, and moved his expensive import into the last available parking space. As he angled it in, a new, also imported, four-wheel-drive vehicle rounded the corner from the opposite direction. Although he was somewhat distant, he wanted the space, too. The first gentleman locked his car and started to walk away as the second approached the area. To his horror, the second fellow rammed his fine car, backed up, and rammed it again and again, ruining both new vehicles. But in so doing, the aggressor became the *vivo* and, to his distorted values, made a *bobo* of the other. Now imagine a whole country run on these principles.

Super highways in the United States are a source of amazement to American ex-pats who come back on furlough. Overseas, we fuss a lot about narrow, winding, potholed roads which are slower than winter molasses and blocked with humans used as pack animals. To go more than five miles an hour is often impossible. American roads, by comparison, are under-utilized except during rush hours.

Where an in-town road in a developing Asian country is solidly lined with little houses and shops, the street becomes the meeting and visiting place of the people. There are no sidewalks, so they walk in the street and push carts to pick up garbage or sell hot meals. Cars try to weave around pedicabs or the somewhat faster motorcycle-powered cabs and the randomly parked cars.

Most streets are one-way, so you have to learn separate routes for going and for coming back. This also means that the traffic is constantly driving in circles to get back to where they couldn't turn off, or simply making three consecutive right turns to effect a left turn. The reverse is true if the English got there first and left all the cars driving on the wrong side of the road.

The directional signal levers get changed, too. My teenagers used to hoot and howl when I flipped the windshield wipers wanting a left turn signal. But they learned to drive in Indonesia, and I got the last laugh when they started driving in the United States.

In 1967, there were only about 5,000 cars in all of Saudi Arabia. A few years later, cars choked the city streets and

Brief Transition from Camel Driving to Car Driving

stalled the capitol city with snarled traffic. In the 1980's on Riyadh's Sitteen Street (so named because it was sixty meters wide), when the traffic was blocked, taxis drove on the sidewalk.

At traffic lights, the cars would line up in racing form, wedged into every crack, revved to go at the first blink of green. My husband called this "driving like a jelly bean" because it reminded him of how the little candies would fill up all the spaces in the Easter baskets of his childhood.

Driver's licenses were given for filling out a form and paying a fee, not for driver proficiency. Men came off camels and into cars, trying to drive as if there were no difference.

Since women by law cannot drive at all in Saudi Arabia, we had to hire men to take us daily through the very jaws of death. These drivers had no driver education, no defensive driver training, and no experience in an automobile culture.

There is only occasional driver testing in Indonesia today, but women can get a license and drive. We use drivers a lot because a driver at a salary of $250 a month can make one car work for a family like two, whereas buying another standard, medium-sized Toyota would cost about $35,000 and require another $2,000 per annum insurance premium. A good driver saves mom many hours of being locked in this ghastly traffic once she learns how to take advantage of having a "gofer" in her employ.

Still, it is often convenient to be able to drive within the neighborhood, to the nearest grocery store, and on Sunday afternoons when the kids want to be delivered to a friend's house. We Americans usually take a little time to get used to driving on the left side of the road and getting over the fear of hitting a cart, pedicab, or a family on the rough, narrow streets lined with sewer ditches. Your home country license is good for ninety days, and then you need an Indonesian one. That way, when you are stopped for some reason or no reason, the cash-on-the-spot "fine" is lower.

Jeannie left the Indonesian highway department the proud possessor of a new technicolor driver's license. Her driver was waiting in the parking lot which was in the thickest of the awful driving area of town, so she let him continue at the wheel. He asked her how much it cost her to get the license. She was feeling a bit guilty because it was just a big paper drill with no test. The expediter had gotten her to the head of the line when hundreds of people had been milling about and waiting for their names to be called.

Jeannie didn't want to admit how much she had paid to walk out with a license in just over an hour. He asked again, and she admitted she had written a check for about ninety dollars.

"Ha!" he exclaimed. "I have a friend working there. He got me a license for thirty dollars!" She was uncomfortable about the money, and even more so because she trusted the lives of her family to a driver who had never had a driver's test.

Never mind, the traffic rules are largely unwritten. You just have to have The Right Stuff.

The truth is, if a car belonging to a foreigner is ever in a wreck, in most emerging countries the fault of the wreck will be assigned to the foreigner and he will pay all damages. The reasoning is infallible: if the foreigner had stayed in his own country, the wreck wouldn't have happened.

When my wreck finally happened in Saudi Arabia—the one I had lived in dread of from the first day—the fault was declared to be my driver's for a really creative reason. We were on a wide, paved, divided road, crossing a narrow, comparatively insignificant dirt road. Neither had a light nor sign, and visibility was blocked by the ever-present six foot high wall around someone's property. The police said the dirt road had the right of way over the four lane divided street because the dirt road had been there longer. I thought it may have had something to do with the fact that the other car was owned by one of the two thousand or so Saudi princes.

Quite a number of international companies strongly discourage their families from driving in the more difficult places overseas. The legal entanglements can be unfortunate when a "rich" foreigner hits/is hit by a local citizen. The wealthier wrecker/wreckee will pay, without a doubt. Why do we drive, then? I think it has something to do with control. You can only sit in the back seat so long before the need explodes within you to grab the steering wheel, point the air conditioner vents your way, and experience the freedom of the road—if you can find a space wide enough to get the car though.

Funny Food

The real adventure in travel is food. I've known this ever since the sixth grade, when my teacher Mrs. McMurphy told of her whirlwind trip one week through Europe. She had eggs for breakfast in London and flew to Paris, where she thought *oeuff* sounded interesting for lunch. That night they were in Germany, where she picked the word *eier* from the menu. That is, she ate eggs all three meals that day when she could have had the most exciting food Europe has to offer!

The cook in a certain construction camp in the Arabian desert, four hours by taxi from the nearest airport, always does his best to make the visiting *sahids* (gentlemen) welcome. The visitors on a given evening have long since shucked their ties and suit jackets and have loosened their collars. They sit on the floor and eat with their right hands (because the left is unclean), and grin and bite into goat meat so tough that it must be worked like jerky until the jaws scream in defeat. To show their pleasure in the feast laid out for them, they accept and eat the food served to them—in the Bedouin custom one never serves himself—and finally they lean back and belch loudly to proclaim their satisfaction.

It is not at all unusual for businessmen to tell of being royally feted with parts of animals they would not have ordered for themselves. Being given the eye of the goat is an honor which simply cannot be declined.

Our friend Christopher told of being seated at the head of the table when the dinner served was a very rare and costly seafood to which he was extremely allergic. Being a sensitive and diplomatic person, he put the feelings of his host above his comfort and ate it with much gusto—and then excused himself to the men's room to throw the toxic food back up.

Monkey meat is still a delicacy in some third-world Asian countries. Our friend Rodney was honored at a dinner where a monkey was placed under a table with a circular hole in it, and just the top of the monkey's head was fitted into the hole. One strong sweep with a sharp machete cut the top of the monkey's head off and the brain was served to Rodney before the monkey even knew he was dead. Then the barbeque began.

Sometimes it is not the food which is the adventure so much as the way in which it is served. I still don't care to crunch through shrimp, shell and all, as they do in Indonesia and Brazil, for example.

At a large dinner party where guests were scattered informally all about the house, a British hostess in Saudi Arabia served a salad of raw shrimp. One of the guests who loved shrimp—but couldn't face them raw—had not had shrimp for a very long time. She slipped the few shrimp out of her salad serving into a paper napkin and thus into her purse, took them home, and cooked and ate them the next day.

After successful negotiations concerning a major shrimp company in the Far East, the account manager was delighted to be taken to a fine restaurant owned by the company, to eat the very best shrimp in the world. The owner of the company ordered for everyone. Lobster-sized live shrimp were brought to the table in a copper chafing dish, in a sauce fragrant with garlic, onions, and spices. Brandy was poured over them and ignited, and a lid was placed over the scrambling crustaceans. When the kicking settled down, the lid

Shrimp Don't Get Any Fresher

was lifted and the shrimp were served onto the plate. They don't get any fresher than that.

When you have lived for a long time in a country with good quality control over its foods, you make certain assumptions that may not be valid elsewhere. The United States, the land of great breakfasts, makes so many good cereals. A narrow selection of these are exported to faraway places, where they are sold for high prices. In the 1970's a box of cereal sold for ten dollars in Riyadh, Saudi Arabia. But the children had been begging for the chocolate cereal that "all their friends ate" and I had been too miserly to buy. I gave in. I bought the ten dollar cereal and served it to my precious grammar schoolers, and what did the ungracious children do? They sat there stirring it, claiming that it had bugs in it. "Impossible," said I. "I just bought it yesterday and opened it this moment. Now eat your cereal. The school bus will be here in a few minutes."

They ate slowly, distrustfully, and left for school. I sat down with my coffee, irritated that I had spent ten dollars and they hadn't appreciated it. They had poured a lot of milk in the bowl, too, and had left it with a little bit of the chocolate cereal floating in it. No, SWIMMING in it. The chocolate cereal was SWIMMING in the milk! Yuck! I had made my little darlings eat bugs for breakfast!

It's surprising sometimes which foods are regarded as precious to an individual homemaker. I always brought back from summer vacation a can of Ocean Spray Cranberry Sauce with Whole Berries. At times I've spent up to sixty-five dollars for a small frozen turkey, but we had an all-American-really-grateful Thanksgiving dinner with prayers and hymns every year. I was always ready with my can of cranberry sauce.

Vickie had a can of cherry pie filling that she moved with her household goods through five African and Middle Eastern countries. She never used it; it was her security blanket. She knew that wherever she lived, she could have a cherry pie in just a few minutes. And Jane will use her precious little freezer space in Brazil to preserve a box of American white cake mix for up to five years, or until the replacement comes in someone's suitcase.

While most countries have some variety of powdered sugar for use in icings and desserts, none is so fine and smooth as the American confectioner's sugar. Icings of plain sugar are either gritty or else they are cooked and whipped. This explains the foreign cake icings of jam, cream, and sweetened condensed milk. So in order to have a truly American layer cake, we need to bring in the snowy white, soft and powdery confectioner's sugar.

Mary Jane moved to Brazil without knowing this, and so she asked her nineteen year old son to bring in some confectioner's sugar when he came home from college at Christmas. His passage through customs was going well, despite the usual suspicion of male youths, until the powdered sugar was discovered. The young man had found a bargain on powdered sugar in a U.S. supermarket. It came by the pound in clear bags with little marking, instead of the familiar box.

The customs officers thought they had found that rare exception—an American teenager smuggling drugs *into* South America. The parents waited outside the customs area while all the passengers came through except their son. More customs agents came in. The young man, who spoke no Spanish or Portuguese, finally realized what the agents' excitement was about, and broke out in a cold sweat. He produced his father's business card and asked them to call the office to speak with his father's secretary in Portuguese to clarify the situation. The agents weren't interested. He tried to open one of the bags and eat some of the powder to prove it was harmless sugar, but people have done that before and have died. They would not allow him to eat it.

The customs agents were preparing to handcuff him and take him off to jail when help arrived. A Brazilian expediter, hired to ensure that all the visa paperwork went well, had accompanied the parents to the airport. When the young man did not arrive in a reasonable amount of time, the expediter entered the "no entry" area with a smile and nod to the guards, and went upstream to the customs area. With a lot of fast talking and very efficient manner, he extracted the young man and his luggage from the customs area, leaving behind the suspicious substance and a lot of telephone numbers. The expediter once again had earned his fee and friends for life.

The year that we moved from Argentina to Indonesia, I put American Halloween candies in a small add-on shipment from the States. Months went by before the shipment arrived, though, and Halloween was long past when we unpacked in Indonesia. The candy remained in hiding, and the children never knew it was there. A couple of months later we were having good friends over for dinner, and I had been too busy to fix a proper dessert. It would be a special treat, I rationalized, and so pretty to serve the brightly colored, lovingly imported M & M's in the little white china bowls. A finger-food dessert. How imaginative of me. How generous to share with our friends what could not be bought within a thousand miles.

When the tiny black ants from the candy ran across the white china, I thought my eyes were going funny. Then I prayed that only my M & M's had ants. Not so. Everyone was staring into their white bowls and not eating. Naturally, the younger child wailed, "Mom, there's ANTS in my candy!" And my gracious guest, ever in control while I sat aghast, hopped up and gathered all the little bowls, saying that we would just freeze the candy and the frozen ants would be easy to separate from the candy later. We went on with coffee as if nothing had gone wrong. The candy was never mentioned again.

Our family was stranded in Cairo in Christmas of 1978 when the flight from Riyadh was too late to connect with the flight to Paris. Instead of a gastronomic superlative on the Champs Eliseés, we dined with free airline vouchers in the airport restaurant.

We sat for some time before we could get a waiter to bring a menu, although there were few guests dining. This was good, actually, because it gave us time to absorb the situation. We were at the only clean table in the restaurant. The dirty dishes of earlier diners were left piled on the tables. Cats roamed the restaurant. When the cats hopped up on the uncleared tables to eat scraps, other diners threw bread rolls at them from across the room and laughed loudly at the sport.

We were very hungry, and this was the only meal option. The children had been told that they could order anything they wanted because it was on the airline, but we changed our minds. We carefully chose foods that had to be done fresh and were most likely to be safe, like fried eggs and toast. Our field report from Cairo: We ate, we slept, we left.

We have always had a tendency to indulge in delicious foods when traveling. A few years ago, when there was a Pan Am, they advertised their comfortable planes with the slogan "Fly the wide bodies around the world." We have followed their bidding quite literally. So it is certainly not from a holier-than-thou position that the next story is told:

Brazil has a type of restaurant called a *churrascaria* in which waiters circulate with sizzling grilled meats on long spears. Each waiter slices portions for all the guests, returning the meat to the fire in the kitchen and picking up another sword-load of succulent meat as necessary. At all times, several types of meat and many different cuts of beef are being served. There is also a large open buffet of salads and various other foods. So for one price, the guests may eat a little or a lot. The meat keeps coming until or unless you absolutely insist that you don't want any more. If you are obviously enjoying the meats, you will have to fight the waiters off.

In 1991, a worldwide ecology conference was held in Brasilia. Among the thousands of attendees were three Japanese delegates who went to a *churrascaria* one evening. Beef is very expensive in Japan, and is usually eaten in small quantities, so it was a treat to have unlimited servings of excellent quality beef at a low price. The men truly enjoyed their dinners, and kept accepting slices from the enthusiastic waiters. Most *churrascarias* have a wooden disc or hour-glass shape painted red on one end and green on the other, so that the diner can indicate that he wishes for the waiters to either stop or continue serving. Perhaps the three Japanese delegates did not know how to refuse further servings, but they really ate a lot that night.

They paid up and rolled out to the taxi, returned to their hotel and lay in misery, unable to sleep for the pain. When it became apparent that the situation was actually dangerous, they called the front desk attendant, who called an ambulance. They were carted off to a hospital, where their stomachs were pumped. Their humiliation became public when the story was printed in the newspaper the next morning.

I think about them every time I eat at a *churrascaria*, and I wish them well in the land of rice and dried salted fish.

Reverse Culture Shock

Culture Shock is a term invented to describe the difficulty in adjusting to a new life situation in a foreign place. It may surprise those who have not had the experience of moving back home after living abroad, but reverse culture shock, or re-entry shock, carries a big whammy. When you are in a foreign place, you can always tell yourself that this is only temporary, this is not my home country, and I can go home if it becomes unbearable. But when you go home you may find that

A) your home country isn't as perfect as you remembered;

B) a lot of adjustment is necessary to fit back in; and

C) somebody fast-forwarded the world while you were gone.

Life in an emerging country can be very difficult, so the companies who move us around will do a lot to ease the strain. Most provide maintenance for their employees' homes and appliances. We cost our institutions a lot of money, and the executive should not be using his time in manual labor. Our companies also don't want the wife and family to force the executive to pull out because they can't cope with bad plumbing and wiring, walls that crack open, lights that won't light and freezers that don't freeze. But when you go back home, you're on your own.

Having a full-time maid is wonderful. Think of it: I only clean toilets when I'm on vacation. I could do without ironed underwear (to prevent the culture of disease) and ironed sheets, but I have really missed the live-in baby-sitter and dishwasher when the children were young. Reverse Culture Shock? We're talking Real World Re-entry here.

Upon their return home, ex-pats from the Developed World are often stunned by the opulence and availability of every material want or need. Having lived with the daily threat of street robbery, we are amazed to see men and women in the United States doing routine shopping errands with layers of gold on every body part from which it will hang.

Imagine the shock when a missionary to the desert country of Pakistan returned to the United States for a brief summer visit, and went to a shopping mall with her mother in a major mid-western city. Hearing water flowing, she followed the sound to the center of the mall and discovered a fountain cascading from the height of thirty feet in beautiful patterns of light and water. She stood in awe, and tears began to stream down her cheeks as she watched the abundant, crystal clear dancing water. Her mother feared she needed to be committed.

Just a few years ago, there were many desert countries that had never had ice cream. (Even now, there is a lot of ice cream sold that has been thawed and re-frozen several times and would be considered unfit for consumption back home.) How do you describe ice cream to a child who has never seen it, nor eaten fresh cream? One mother had told her little children about the sweet, smooth stuff, and how they were going to love it when they got home for vacation. She bought them each a cone at her first opportunity, which was from a street vendor in New York City. Instead of relishing it, the little ones stood on the summer sidewalk and cried. They didn't like it. It was cold. It hurt their teeth. The mother was dumbfounded. It was unnatural not to like ice cream.

A favorite story in our family is about watermelon. It had never occurred to me that our little girl didn't know about watermelon. We had gone camping and fishing with the Carver family in Oklahoma, and Grandpa had bought a big, ripe water-melon to cut at lunch time. All the time we were fishing in the river, the watermelon was sitting in the cool shallows waiting for cutting time. Kelly had heard us talk about that watermelon all morning. At last, Grandpa carried it from the river's edge to the picnic table and got out the big knife. As he pierced it, the melon cracked open in perfect, succulent ripeness. Grandpa cut a long wedge and set the first piece in front of Kelly. The light in her eyes at seeing the beautiful red slice dimmed, however, when she noticed the black seeds. Instead of digging in, she asked, "Mommy, do I have to eat the raisins?"

People who have lived in relative hardship tend to remember the home country with a perfection that it cannot possibly live up to. I mean, *people take baths in drinking water* back home.

I was so fed up in Saudi Arabia with phones without dial tones, lost mail, and power outages, which meant no air conditioning in 130 degree heat. On our first night of vacation at my parents' home in Mobile, Alabama, a bad thunderstorm came up. An enormous bolt of lightning struck near the house and all the power went off. I stood there in the pitch blackness laughing convulsively that this could happen in America. In three minutes the power was all back on, and the alarm my reaction had caused Mother brought me back down. Sanity is such a fragile thing, yes?

And then there was the year that our return to Saudi Arabia had to be delayed, so I put the children in elementary school in my home town for a six weeks. Within days, our daughter came home with a form letter from the school nurse that head lice had been found on one of the students, and we were all to inspect our children and take precautions. Head lice? In America?

One summer we flew all night and all the next day from Riyadh to Mobile, changing time by eight hours. As soon as we were rested, we drove from Mobile to Jackson, Mississippi, where an uncle was having a birthday party. The family gathered at Morrison's Cafeteria and took a large table off to the side, all talking at once and hugging each other. As the meal progressed, our son, then about seven years old, tugged at my sleeve.

"Mom, are we in America?"

"Yes, son. We flew to America and then we drove to the state of Mississippi, which is beside Alabama. We're still in America."

The meal continued, the whole family laughing, speaking with the exaggerated drawl of the deep south, swapping family tales. Quinn again gently tugged again at my sleeve.

"Mom, do these people speak English?"

Sally, living on an Asian island, received a call from her daughter Katy in college back in Texas.

"Mom," she whimpered, "I had a wreck. It isn't too bad, but the right fender is messed up."

"Are you okay, honey?"

"Yes, I'm fine," Katy replied.

"Did you call the insurance company?"

"Sure, Mom. I've already called and they are being really nice about it."

"Don't worry, then. If you are able to drive the car, go on to your classes. We'll talk again when you know more."

Ten hours passed. The phone rang again.

"Mom," Katy sobbed. "I had another wreck! I was just sitting at a traffic light and this guy crashed into me."

Sally learned that the daughter was not injured and was calling from her home. But none of the usual assurances were calming Katy. Out of control now, she wailed, "Mom, I don't want to go to jail!"

Katy had been reared all over the world, and she *knew* that when a wreck happens, the police take both victims and witnesses to jail until the matter is resolved and the paperwork done. "They didn't arrest me after the first wreck this morning, but I'm sure they must be coming for me now!"

Sally tried to talk Katy down, but feared that her precious daughter was close to a nervous breakdown. She flew a day and a half to be at Katy's side, and to assure her that things aren't done that way in the U.S.A.

The reverse culture shock involved in ground transportation alone strikes on a lot of levels, like a long good-news, bad-news joke. Our home countries have beautiful, wide-open highways. There is a wonderful array of cars to buy without paying a 200% import tax. But you have to do your own shopping, fetching, and car-pooling. On the other hand, it's a relief not to have the driver sitting around in the garage smoking and playing cards with the guard, gardener, or houseboy until his next errand.

There's such freedom in being able to hop in a car and drive to a supermarket with lots of free parking and no little boys to "guard" the car or direct you in how to park it, even if they have never been inside a car in their lives.

The supermarket has every imaginable food attractively arranged along wide aisles, safely refrigerated, enticingly displayed. The stock boys and butchers are clean and the checkers smile and ask how you are. I don't care if they don't care. It's much nicer than a recalcitrant snarl.

Instead of picking the lesser of evils to cook for supper, you're picking the best available. The cans, boxes, bottles, and bags tell you what's in them—all the ingredients, chemicals, and calories. It probably indicates my degree of reverse culture shock that I want to read it all, choose from all the brands, and just savor the magic of going to a modern supermarket. It's like stepping into a time machine and being dropped into the shiny, fragrant future with elevator music swirling in the background.

Another aspect of culture shock is the awareness of safety considerations. We are stunned when we see, in fairly modern countries, people welding without eye protection, jack-hammering with no ear coverage, broken tiles waiting to trip pedestrians and holes left unguarded in the sidewalk of a major city, and every manner of sharp object sticking out to cut or scrape. Then we come home and learn that lawsuits are being won for hundreds of thousands of dollars when the plaintiff was simply not using common sense in some situation that is much safer than what we live with every day overseas. We read of the family of a man winning a wrongful death suit when he, in a drunken stupor, climbed a fence, ignored large warning signs, and fell onto an electrified railway and was electrocuted. Most of the world doesn't have such a fence, and when drunks die breaking the law, no one sues. The Developed World and Emerging World seem to exhibit opposite excesses.

Our family temporarily returned to life in the United States after four years in a country which said it granted us religious freedom, but in fact made free worship as difficult as possible. All American children learn that the United States was founded with religious freedom as a basic right, but few have experienced the alternative. So when we went to church in the United States, I had to deal with my feelings that Americans were not grateful enough and did not take the privilege seriously enough. Some churches seemed too much a social group and a Sunday fashion show to please me. For once I kept my mouth shut and did not insult others with what I thought they thought. I wrestled very quietly with a personal form of reverse culture shock.

Sometimes I ask people who have visited the United States for the first time what surprised them most. One answer is the unexpected presence of multiple races and how the various groups work out their relationships inside one country. Chile and Argentina, for example, don't have any sizable minority races. Other countries may have one race legally or effectively subjugated to another.

In Jamaica only a few years ago, the superior positions were all occupied by whites. The school principals were white, the governor of Jamaica, the bank president, and most of the wealthy people were whites. All the menial work was done by blacks. So when a young Jamaican black man came to New York City and saw a street sweeper who was white, it blew his mind. This became a turning point in how he felt about his own potential.

Each move is a chance to grow personally. Hopes and insecurities rise to the surface at a life juncture. Things you thought were buried years ago and things you never knew were there jostle for a place beside strengths developed in the past.

All the skills and all the handicaps are put in motion in the new direction. It's a unique sort of self-test that we put ourselves through. We learn under stress what can not be learned in an easy chair life. It's never dull, but it's sometimes painful.

It's a Small World

A charming young man, Samuel J. Beauregard, was living and working in a foreign country. His family lived in a fine house rented for them by his company, and he drove a fine car. The ex-pat community gradually got to know him better, and learned of the aristocratic background of the Beauregards in his home state. He shared with friends the details of his noble parentage, and told of the magnificent white house on the hill just outside the town where he had been reared.

Eventually, one of his new friends was traveling and happened to meet a stranger from the same small town in Virginia.

"You're from Frog Hollow, Virginia? Then you must know my new friend, Sam Beauregard," he happily exclaimed. "He's from a well-to-do family that lives in a fine white house on a hill overlooking your town."

"Well, yes, of course I know the Beauregard family. I grew up with the Beauregard boys. But they are not a particularly well-to-do family." Further conversation revealed that the Beauregard aristocracy was fictional. The family manse was more like a white shack on a dirt road that did, after all, go uphill.

The truth slowly spread like little ripples on a pond, and Sam looked foolish every time he dropped his broad hints about being a branch of the old southern aristocracy. He never knew why, but some of his new acquaintances were no longer interested in cultivating his friendship. In all fairness to his turned-off new friends, the loss of face was not because he was not blue-blooded, but because he had mis-represented himself.

Or consider this Small World story: A lovely couple, Mr. and Mrs. Wayne Donner, moved to Indonesia from the previous posting in England. They quickly began to settle in and make themselves known socially. The wife, Tina, was a beautiful woman of oriental descent, somewhat younger than Wayne, and she obviously adored him. She was close by his side every minute.

About two months passed, and another couple moved to Indonesia from England. The new lady had heard that the Wayne Donners were going to be at a party at the American Club, and she was anxious to see them again.

"Ah, there's Wayne now, and his wife Tina is standing right next to him," said the innocent bystander.

"Yes, that's Wayne all right. But his wife's name is Martha, and she's a tall blond. They have two children in college. And they are not divorced."

The moral of this story is that England is not far enough away from Indonesia to pull this kind of trick. One can't *get* far enough away to try this one!

A most remarkable series of events just occurred in São Paulo, Brazil. The story exploded and then continued to open like a deadly flower as the recently uncensored, gossip-hungry press bent back the petals day by day.

There was a trial under way in São Paulo which con-cerned kick-backs and bribes in a Brazilian province. The trial was not going well for the accused, and the governor of the province was subpoenaed to testify against him. The governor was lodged in a hotel the night before he was to testify, with his bodyguard on duty in an adjoining room.

An American arrived in São Paulo to do business, knowing nothing of this drama, and was given the room on the other side of the governor. Very late that night, two masked gunmen forced their way into the American's room, tied him up and robbed him. After they left, he heard a shot in the governor's room. The governor's bodyguard had been trying to stay awake by watching television. The shot jolted him awake, but it seemed to fit into the plot of the TV movie, so he settled back into sleep. The American wiggled and squirmed until he got his mouth uncovered and one big toe loose, and he attempted to contact the front desk by telephone. Wouldn't you know it, no one would answer. Not the operator, not the front desk, nobody. He was afraid to scream out in the hotel, lest the robbers return and kill him as they had threatened. But international direct dialing is wonderful. Carefully punching the buttons with his big toe, he called his home number in the States, and his wife answered the phone.

He explained his predicament, giving her the name and address of the hotel in Brazil and his room number. She called the police in their home city, who called the state police, who called the F.B.I., who called the São Paulo police, who came to the hotel and rescued him. At some point in the ruckus following, the non-guarding bodyguard woke up and checked on the governor and found him shot to death. The police deduced that the robbery of the American was only a ruse to tie and gag him so that, if he heard the gunshot, he couldn't report it.

BUT—the São Paulo police were quick to notice that the executive had been tied up with pantyhose.

"Where did the pantyhose come from?" they wanted to know.

At first he pretended not to know. Maybe they had been found under the bed, left by a previous guest. Then he confessed, man-to-man (surely the police would understand) that he had had a "friend" in the room earlier that evening. The police were relentless, since a murder had been committed which thwarted a major criminal case. He had to give the name of the young woman.

The police contacted her, and all the information was going to newspaper reporters on an hour-by-hour basis. The

International Direct Dialing a Rescue

young woman loved the publicity, and told all. She and a
girlfriend had both been with the American in his room earlier the night of the robbery and murder. He *usually* called
them when he was going to be in town. They had met him
according to plans, had been down to the coast with him,
then back to the hotel room. One of the women had accidentally left without her pantyhose. When the murderers
broke in, they found just the perfect thing with which to tie
him up.

This businessman had a very important job with his
company which required him to travel extensively through-
out the world. Police investigation revealed that the local
branch employees of the company knew his reputation for

117

having a woman or two in all the cities where he traveled to work. And his wife read it all in the newspapers. It's a small world, after all.

A multinational company hired a fine group of recruits to its officer level, and began to put them through in-house training at the head office in New York City. The young recruits were smart, they were motivated, they had new master's degrees, and many of them were single. This group contained a single woman of considerable beauty and charm who shall be called Jill. Of the men in the class, Frank began to be a special friend. They studied together often, had apartments in the same building, and sometimes walked home from work together. In due time, their compatibility extended to shared dinners and movies.

One day, walking back to their apartments together, Jill and Frank stopped to admire an oriental carpet displayed in a store window. It was lovely. It was a Friday night and they had time, so they decided to go into the store and find out how much the carpet cost. The salesman went into high gear, found out Frank Forster's name, and assumed that they were married. He went through the whole sales routine calling them "Mr. and Mrs. Forster." They were amused, and didn't correct his mistake.

Both Jill and Frank liked the carpet, but either one would have let the other buy it. But then a remarkable thing happened. They liked the "Mr. and Mrs. Forster" sales pitch. They decided to get married and buy the carpet.

Jill and Frank Forster had a grand wedding and the company sent them off together to a country in the Middle East for their first jobs as new officers. They were successful in their jobs, but something was missing in their marriage. They continued to be friends, and yet they were just never in love. Whatever that is, it didn't happen.

Sadly, they grew apart instead of growing together. About three years passed, and Jill found herself tremendously attracted to James, a handsome professional who worked at the same company. When he was transferred to the Far East, he invited her to divorce Frank and transfer with him and marry him. Frank was a very good sport about the whole thing, and the plans were made but few people knew.

In order to avoid scandal if possible, James moved to the orient on schedule and Jill began the divorce process quietly. She eventually let people know that she was transferring, but Frank would be staying.

A farewell party was given in Jill's honor, and a collection was taken up for a gift. The amount contributed for the lovely, popular lady was rather large, and a nice gift was purchased. And so it was that her marriage to Frank began and ended with an oriental carpet.

Life under Glass

Joyce was grocery shopping in Jakarta one morning, and heads turned as she pushed her cart through the narrow aisles. *I must look really good today,* she thought. Although the tropical city is informal, she had done her hair nicely, had applied a full routine of make-up, and was even wearing pantyhose. The stock boys and clerks noticed her, and many were smiling or even laughing, which is so normal in Indonesia that it can mean anything or nothing.

Joyce was enjoying the attention, until a female clerk pointed out, as gently as possible, that her skirt and slip were tucked into the waist of her pantyhose, and her bottom was revealed. Joyce weighed 247 pounds then, and she was so embarrassed that she abandoned her grocery cart and got out of the store as quickly as possible. Joyce told this story on herself after she had lost, and kept off, eighty pounds.

Living overseas may give the ex-pat the sensation of conducting a life under glass, in full view of the curious local population. The more physically different you appear, the more you feel noticed or even watched as you move about.

Worse yet, a citizen of a developed country living in an emerging country is generally assumed to be rich. Depending on many factors beyond our control, we may be envied and generically hated, or we may be treated with particular respect and deference, which makes us vulnerable to developing pride. Pride, in turn, can lead people into silly situations with the local population looking on. Just when you think you're really sumpthin', you're ready for a fall.

The first time we were invited to the Buenos Aires American Club for a dinner honoring the American Ambassador, I felt so important. If they could only see me back home, I thought, dining with the Ambassador and his wife. I wore a beautiful dress of blue georgette, its full skirt swishing as I walked.

During the cocktail hour, a waiter stepped behind a folded partition and motioned in my direction. Of course, I ignored him. He began to make a little "psst" noise, and it looked as if he were trying to get my attention. Being a lady, I of course ignored him harder. He went away. I wondered what he wanted, but the señora doesn't talk to waiters behind a folded screen.

In a few minutes he was back, and it was clear that the "psst" was for me. He was waving enormous, shiny scissors and pointing to the bottom of my luscious dress. At the waiter's insistence, I stepped just out of view of the other cocktail-sipping, gaily chatting guests. He showed me that a large white dry cleaner's tag hung from the hem of my dress on a four inch white string. With all care and modesty, he bent down and clipped the string and handed me the tag. I rejoined the party somewhat humbled. Now I know to look for unusual tags in strange places from foreign dry cleaners. I've also had a necessary attitude adjustment.

Genie was a trim, beautiful American woman who took up jogging in Jakarta. She looked great in her cute little jogging shorts early every morning. She liked to run with other women when she could find someone willing, but you would be able to recognize her in any group: she was the one with a full face of make-up.

The year-round humid summer climate of Jakarta naturally encourages the population to conserve energy. There are some excellent athletes, to be sure, but the average Indonesian does not have the custom of doing heavy exercise. As Genie's range increased, it became harder to find runners who wanted to run as far as she.

An Indonesian woman named Inda had asked Genie several times if they might run together. The answer was always "yes," but it hadn't happened yet.

Finally they made firm plans. "Let's run from our neighborhood to my club," Inda proposed. "I know a good route. It's a nice distance for me."

It was a good jog, but about half of what Genie expected. They got water at the club and rested just a minute. Then Inda said she was ready to take the city bus home.

"Take the bus? I thought we were going to jog back. I didn't bring any money," said Genie.

"That's okay, I'll loan you some," offered Inda.

"But I can't get on a city bus in my wet jogging outfit. I'll get arrested," said Genie. Indonesia is a modest country with an Islamic tradition. Women do not get on a city bus in jogging shorts.

"My friend lives close to here," said Inda. "We'll go to her house and borrow a skirt for you."

So they found a simple skirt that Genie could pull on over her jogging shorts, and the two ladies boarded the city bus instead of jogging back home.

The bus stop for Inda came before Genie's. As she was about to get off, she turned to Genie and said, "Give me the skirt now, and I'll get it back to my friend."

Observed by a bus load of staring Indonesians, Genie had to stand up and take off the borrowed skirt. And Inda wondered why Genie never wanted to jog to her club any more.

The Tower of Babel

Patricia, an American homemaker living in Indonesia, went to buy an electric curling iron when she had just arrived and barely knew the basics of the language. As she held out her index finger and used the few words she did know—"long," "hot," and "hard"—the young salesgirl backed off with a horrified look. Playing the game of "shopper's charades" with her hands, hair, and available props, Patricia finally got the girl to understand. She quickly bought the curling iron and left. Actually, she wanted to buy a blow dryer, too, but could only imagine to what conclusions the girl might jump if she had tried that one.

The study of foreign languages is fascinating once you get past the grammar book and into real life. It is frequently the ex-pat wife who becomes functional in a new language before the husband if she is dealing with shopping, plumbers and electricians, maids and traffic. The husband in the typical ex-pat family spends his day in the workplace with a good bilingual secretary while the wife is trying to learn the word for celery, where to buy it and how to get there. She develops a more practical vocabulary and learns how to talk around the words and expressions she hasn't studied yet.

Soon the businessman may be negotiating contracts in the new language but not know the word for "fork" or how to say "fill 'er up" at the gas station. It is very common for both partners to study hard for a little while, and then settle into familiar patterns and coast.

Shopping in a new country with a new language requires courage. The ex-pat has to be willing to try words looked up in a dictionary, talk to strangers and wave the hands and really try to communicate. Occasionally, you feel so foolish. Sucking in courage, you open the door to a drugstore and hope for a salesperson who will either speak your language or help you speak hers.

In so many nations, you find that it takes four people to sell a simple bubble pack of aspirin: place your order here, get it filled there, pay for it where the clerk is behind the glass shield, and collect the aspirin from the one who wrapped it. The cashier will mumble for you to give exact change, and the wrapper will want the receipt from the cashier, both using words that were not in the first five language lessons. You need a flow chart and fifteen minutes to buy aspirin even if you are the only customer in the store. That's the system. By the time you leave with your purchase, you feel you have earned it. Okay, you got the aspirin. Now how do you say "toothbrush?"

An unsophisticated, backwater Louisiana woman had just moved to Indonesia. Her husband had told her that the reason the Indonesian women were so beautiful was because they had some kind of secret product which they used. Naturally, she wanted to find out what the secret product was and get some for herself. One day she was shopping in a drug store and saw a small package with the brand name "Wrinkles." That was it! She was sure she had found it! Excitedly, and perhaps a bit loudly, she fired questions at the salesgirl, who could speak English but could hardly understand this accent. "Is it good? Does it work? How many times do you use it?" she asked.

The girl backed away, as if under attack, slowly shaking her head, and said only one word: "Condoms."

Language acquisition comes with much practice. Some sensational errors can be made learning a language which does not routinely use any form, any tense, of the verb "to be," as in Arabic, Indonesian, and many others. (That is, there ain't no "is," "was," or "will be.") At first, it seems impossible to get around such a hurdle. In fact, native speakers of these languages sometimes negotiate a meaning through an exchange of questions and answers not only to clarify the facts, but also the tense.

Indonesian, for example, has no conjugation of verbs. The key to the tense is the first word in the sentence, such as *sudah*, which is a flag saying, "What is being said has already happened." Waving the hand back over the shoulder reinforces the flag word for past tense, and motioning in front indicates future tense, *akan*. Sometimes the hands just substitute for the words.

And then there are new and glorious pitfalls in learning Spanish and Portuguese, which have two different verbs for various states and conditions of being. You may wonder how you could have insulted a lady by saying she is beautiful, until you learn that the verb you used implies that she is not usually beautiful but she's fixed up pretty well today. Or laughter could result when you say a building is in a certain place, but you use the verb which indicates that the building is there at this moment, but it moves around a lot. Once again, you vow that you are going to get back to those books you studied so hard for the first three months and have used as dust collectors ever since.

Sign reading becomes an obsession as one breaks in a new language in a new city. Newcomers to Jakarta soon notice the signs indicating that "Doktor Gigi" has offices all over the city. Does this guy sell franchises? Some of the offices look really nice, and others are real dumps. Eventually we learn that "doktor gigi" is the term for "dentist," and that all the signs for that other guy, "Doktor Hewan," mean "veterinarian."

Those who speak Spanish are surprised to see establishments in Brazil labeled "Borracharia." In Spanish, *borracho* means "drunk." So what are these dirty little shops with old tires lying about and unkempt men coming and going? Are they places to get rip-roaring, knee-walking drunk? No, in fact a *borracharia* in Brazil is a tire repair shop.

Likewise, our friend Henry went into a *whiskeria* in Buenos Aires, Argentina, to get a drink after work. To his disappointment, he found that it was a men's shaving parlor.

And then you also see signs which purport to be English. My favorite was at a major intersection in Riyadh, Saudi Arabia, where a language school had set up shop. In red letters three feet tall across the front of the school was the slogan, "LEARN TO SPEAK ENGLISH GOOD."

Also, there's a shoe store in Bali, Indonesia which advertises to tourists and prints on their business cards, "Thank's for your come." Ours is not an easy language to learn.

The most brilliant professional linguist I have ever had the privilege of knowing said that she felt confused and bewildered in Greece, partly because most of the letters were the same but some were totally different. Others represented a different sound than we are accustomed to. The letter "p" should be read "r," and "b" is "v". All over Greece little coffee shops or bars are labeled "tabepna" which is pronounced "taverna." Greeks also use those letters that occurred in your high school geometry and trigonometry books as the names of angles, like ø and ß. It seems very strange to us, but the Greeks can handle it. The words are long and the grammar complex, but the fastest I have ever heard humans speak was the day I witnessed an argument between two Greeks. It was truly amazing.

Learning a language is not only a matter of learning a lot of words and the grammar to put them together, but also the appropriate idiom to use. By idiom we mean a group of words which express something different from what those words may mean singly. For example, the way to say "never mind" in Indonesian is to put together the words which translate as "no what-what." Other favorites are "sleeping policeman," which means "speed bump," and the Portuguese "kiss-flower" for "hummingbird." In a more profound vein, one of the ways in Arabic to call a person a "non-believer" in God is to say that he is "ungrateful."

It is readily apparent that it is not safe to take idioms used in your native tongue and translate them into a new language. Even so, we may trip in the most innocent accident. For instance, an Argentine pastor had noticed that after the last pot luck dinner, the ladies doing the washing up had thrown dirty dish water out the back door, which resulted in mud being tracked into the church. So before dismissing the congregation, he announced in Spanish, "Please don't throw water out the back door of the church." The congregation burst out in shocked laughter. He was told privately that to "throw water" is the idiom for "urinate."

We chuckle with understanding when a visitor to the U.S., offered more food when he has had quite enough to eat, says, "No thanks. I'm all fed up." But I, for one, have done worse in other languages.

My husband and I had been in an intensive study of conversational German in his graduate school, best known by its nickname "Thunderbird." We took the opportunity to visit Germany on the way to his first foreign posting (if you don't count New York City) and stayed for several days in a small hotel owned and operated by a very congenial family. Breakfast was, of course, included. Americans are known around the world for liking a hearty breakfast, so the *frau* added cheese and a boiled egg to the usual bread, jam, butter and coffee. She asked how the breakfast was, and we skipped over the normal reply of "*sehr gut*" and said that it was "*gantz gut,*" because this sounded to us more robustly satisfying.

On the second day, she had added two kinds of cold cuts to all the cheese, bread, jam, butter and coffee. She asked again how the breakfast was, and we, who had wasted nothing, replied "*gantz gut*" with great fervor.

So on the third day we heard her asking our bilingual friend Gerti if she thought we were satisfied with the breakfast, and what more we would like to eat. With Gerti's help we learned that we had been telling her not that breakfast was "very good," but had erroneously given a weaker response that it was "good enough." The dear lady had begun every day wondering what more the hungry Americans could be wanting for breakfast.

There is one idiomatic expression that does not seem to change much in any language, and is in practice worldwide: when a person finishes giving directions for how to go somewhere, the last phrase is "You can't miss it." They all lie. You can.

A beautiful Australian teen-ager moved to Brazil and cried for weeks about her name. When she introduced herself, people laughed and thought she was joking. It had never had a meaning to her before; it was a pretty, rhythmic series of syllables and nothing more. But in Brazil, "Janela Port" sounds almost like "window door."

There are fascinating pieces of research being revealed these days on how the brain works, and much of it has to do with language acquisition. As soon as I am through with my brain, perhaps someone would like to take it out and play with it. I have had the privilege of studying, to some degree or other, nine languages. Eight of these have been used in their appropriate countries, whereas high school Latin was nothing more than brain candy.

Anyone who speaks more than one language observes some strange short-circuits at times, and it makes us wonder how these things happen. For example, you can get locked into the wrong language sometimes, and it is really hard to close the wrong door of the brain and open the correct one. Twice I've entered a restaurant where the music and ambiance were French, and I was inappropriately locked into French—once in Fort Worth, for crying out loud!

Our family had the superb opportunity of learning to ski in Switzerland while on "Rest and Recuperation" trips from Saudi Arabia. Our ski instruction, over three different vacation times, was in French or German or both. Later we had a chance to ski in the United States. I was on top of the mountain all suited up and ready to shove off, when a horrible realization hit me: I don't know how to ski in English. That's silly, of course, but it seemed real at the time.

During the years when I switched between English and Indonesian all day, and between English and Spanish with my South American friends, I had the Spanish-speaking ladies over for coffee. It was excruciatingly difficult to switch between Indonesian and Spanish as I asked the maid to help with the serving. It was as if no bridges had been made between those two languages.

There are many other examples of scrambled languages. If anyone can teach how to keep Portuguese separate from Spanish and use both freely, please come set up a school in Brazil. Until then, a lot of folks like me will keep speaking fluent "Portagnol."

As if separate languages are not difficult enough, each language evolves within various countries where it is used. For instance, the trunk of a car in America is the "boot" in England, and the hood is the "bonnet." We have many idiomatic differences as well. To "knock up" a person in England means simply to go 'round and knock on the door, whereas for at least forty years in America this has meant to impregnate a woman. Therefore, when the Lay Leader of the church congregation in Riyadh, a very proper English gentleman, announced from the pulpit that dear Mrs. Featherwaite was very sick, and we should "all go 'round and knock her up," he did not understand why the Americans in the congregation thought it funny.

Spanish does the same sort of thing. Besides the routine word substitutions, there are perfectly legitimate words which have taken on slang connotations so strong that they cannot be used in the dictionary-correct manner. The conch shell, *concha*, for example, is the Argentine word for the female private parts. So some Argentine men are fond of having their photos made in front of a restaurant in San Juan, Puerto Rico whose name, La Concha, is written in six foot high letters.

The Spanish verb *coger* means "to get, to pick up, to obtain." It is the sort of verb that is very useful to talk around the more specific verbs that the student may not have learned yet. But in Argentina, it cannot be used because it is slang for the performance of the sex act. The slang meaning has completely overtaken the true definition. People are warned about this in Argentine Spanish (*castellano*) lessons, but some people arrive speaking Spanish and don't take the lessons.

So it was that an American wife was working with the plumbers, painters, and electricians in the new residence and would announce to them every day at 5 pm that she was going to the commuter train station to *coger* her husband. Their usual reaction was a blush, a shrug, and a comment of, "Sure, señora, whatever."

We find that in most languages, the angry expletives are the same: profanity, sex words, and excrement words. There are local variations such as casting aspersions on the virtue of one's mother or unmarried sister, but it all boils down to the same thing. Rather than fill pages with the endless stories which depend on sex and excrement words for their punch lines, we accept that these things happen and go on to more pleasant examples.

Another class of language error is the type in which the fledgling in a new language says a word which sounds close to what he means, but has nothing like the same meaning. Countless times I confused the Argentine pronunciations for horse, hair, onion, and brush, asking the hairdresser to wash my horse, comb my onion, and so forth. In Indonesia the words for head and coconut are similar enough that I often said I had a sick coconut (*kelapa sakit*) when I had a headache (*kepala sakit*).

I sympathize with the Indonesian minister who, in his Christmas sermon, told of Mary going to Bethlehem riding on a soybean. He was the same minister who, intending to say, "Now let us pray (*berdoa*)" at the end of the sermon said, "Now let us sin (*berdosa*)."

The Indonesian words *babi, baju,* and *bayi* mean pig, dress, and baby. So when the parishioner asked the missionary wife what she did today, she answered, "I made a baby" instead of "I made a dress." The giggles told her immediately that she had, in fact, made a mistake. Another missionary, congratulating a couple on their newborn child, said, "You have a very sweet pig!"

The words for "cat" and "yellow" are also very close in sound, *kuncing* and *kuning*. A cook was very upset when she thought her employer was asking her to make a cat cake.

Sometimes it takes a little longer to catch on, and especially when servants want to keep their jobs and would do anything to keep the employer happy. An American couple intended to be telling the gardener that the grass (*rambut*) was too long, and should be cut. He had not cut the grass the next day, so the employer told him again. He seemed surprised, but agreed to comply. On the third day the grass still was not cut, and the employer sought out the gardener and sternly ordered him to cut the grass, or so he thought. The gardener pulled off his cap and showed the employer that he had cut his hair (*rumput*) three times already, and he was almost bald!

And then there was the missionary wife in Indonesia who had a lady over for afternoon tea. The sitting area was very stuffy in this year-round summer country, and she was not able to open the window. She called the houseboy and asked him, she thought, to open the window (*jalana*). Instead, she used the word *jandela*, pants, and he left in a huff without assisting her. The more fluent guest caught the error.

Our friend Veronica says that the Turkish words for a loaf of bread and "man" are so similar that she often went to

You Want Me to Make a Cat Cake?

the baker and asked for two hot men. Everyone chuckled, but she got her bread.

Blessings on the dear Indonesian maid who spoke quite a bit of English, and wanted to help her employer learn Indonesian. After the American lady had slaughtered a sentence and felt like giving up (again), the maid gently said, "That's all right, Madam. You can practice on me. I won't laugh."

Well, you do your best to learn a language. You reach out with the new words stretched in the framework of a foreign grammar, you use your hands and all available props, and give it your best shot. In most places in the world, Paris being the exception, your attempt is at least warmly received.

It helps to be able to laugh at yourself. That's what I appreciated so much about the short, round, over-fifty fellow who told this story to the bunch of us on a five minute break at a language school one day: He was seated at the head table of a formal dinner beside a beautiful young woman whose native language was English, and he had just begun English classes. What an opportunity to try it out! They were trying to converse, although he was stumbling about with difficulty. He leaned closer to her, as the room was getting rather noisy, and said, "You must have much passion with me." She quickly drew away, and if she spoke at all it was to the person on her other side.

Now the fellow was thinking, *What did I say? ...much passion. Humm, maybe that's not the right word.* After a good deal of thought, he got her attention again and said, "What I mean to say is, 'You must have much *patience* with me.'"

We students laughed, and he laughed at his own mistake. It's easier that way.

Speaking a Foreign Body Language

Make a circle by placing the thumb and the index finger together. In the United States, this means "okay" or "perfect." In Japan, it means "money," or gestures that something is expensive. In Brazil, with the fingers down and the back of the hand toward someone else, it is an obscene insult.

Recently, an American movie played in Brazil in which, in the final scene before the credits rolled, one of the main characters shot the "perfect" signal to the other. But in Brazil, it was interpreted as an insult which turned around the meaning of the film's last scene one hundred eighty degrees. The Brazilian audience laughed, but may have wondered at this sudden change in the movie's ending.

There are body gestures and positions that are fairly universal, even among the most primitive tribes, such as puffing up the chest in pride and shrugging the shoulders. Then there are others which are peculiar to specific cultures or even the whim of fashion. As such, they may mean different things to different people.

Another example: the thumbs up "okay" is an insult in Australia, but is used in all kinds of positive ways in Brazil.

"How are you?"

"*Tudo bem.*" (Said with the thumb up.) "Everything's great." Or—

Wedging one's car in front of another, the driver questions with the thumb up, meaning, "May I squeeze in ahead of you?"

The second driver, seeing he has no choice anyway except to ram the first guy off the road, smiles and gives him a thumb up, meaning, "Sure, go ahead. I do it all the time myself."

What could be more friendly than a big open-palmed wave? Almost anything, to a Greek. It's roughly equivalent to an Italian ramming his right fist into the air while slapping the left hand down on the right biceps. Try it privately. It's amazingly expressive.

An American man was in an enormous Brazilian supermarket unsuccessfully looking for catsup. A sweet young female clerk offered to help him, but he didn't know the Portuguese expression for "catsup." With a sudden inspiration, he started hitting one fist with the opposite hand as if trying to jar catsup out of a bottle, repeating, "catsup, catsup." This, however, is an obscene sign in Brazil equal to the Italian's fist in the air. The clerk left insulted and a bit frightened by his aggressive behavior. He never found the *molho tomate.*

A young American visiting his family in Brazil had waited by a busy thoroughfare for a taxi for quite some time, when one finally responded to his wave and pulled up. The prospective rider walked toward the taxi just as something tickled his face. He brushed his hand across his cheek without thinking, and the taxi driver raced off in a huff, leaving him bewildered. Then he remembered being told that to brush the beard area was to indicate "that was a close shave," implying that the taxi was a bad driver. The next time a taxi approached, he kept his hand down and got a ride home.

The same hand motion in Argentina is even more harsh: it is the same as calling a person a "barbarian." And flipping the hand beneath the chin used to be a challenge to a fistfight, but is modified nowadays to a milder level of insult. It's still enough to get you into trouble.

Here's another unique Brazilian comment from one driver to another: if a driver has been zipping between cars, switching lanes and dashing in front of other cars, another driver may get his eye when they are stopped at the next traffic light and make sewing motions. That is, the offending driver is accused of "stitching" between cars and traffic lanes.

I've never witnessed this personally, so maybe it is passing out of fashion, but I'm told that a light touch on the earlobe with thumb and forefinger means "the very best," and is frequently used to compliment to a cook. Crossing the hand to the opposite earlobe is an even higher compliment.

Did you ever notice that in pictures of the Russian population on the street, doing the routine things, they are never smiling? We tend to think that is because they are oppressed people, not happy and free as we are. Actually, it is considered bad manners and generally dumb-looking and inane to walk on the street smiling, outside of home and pub. It just isn't done.

The distance between two people in conversation with one another is a cultural factor. Want to have some fun? Watch the pairs at the next international cocktail party you attend. Some pairs are almost in each other's faces, and some stand back a bit. Now find any Latin talking to an American or British person. The Latin wants to be closer, and the other keeps unconsciously backing off. An American can be backed across the room and against the wall or buffet table as the Latin advances inch by inch. Latins may wonder why we are cold, and we may feel they are "pushy." In an effort not to appear uninvolved or emotionally distant, I try to avoid backing off. It helps if I can put on my reading glasses, though, because otherwise my eyes are out of focus.

Notice how some nationalities or cultural groups touch each other in conversation and others don't. The British particularly do not. How do you feel when someone keeps touching your arm or shoulder to make a point in conversation? Or perhaps you are the toucher who feels the other is distant. It makes you wonder what kind of silent messages you give off.

Mothers and daughters or close girlfriends may hold hands as they walk down the city street in some countries. In Arabia, men often hold hands while walking. We were particularly amused at the very common sight of two soldiers, with rifles slung over their shoulders, walking down the sidewalk holding hands. It doesn't necessarily mean anything about their sexual preferences.

In so many cultures, showing the sole of the foot toward a person is an insult to him or her. This was true in our experience in the Middle East, Mediterranean, and Indonesia, so I've gradually come to regard it as safer not to cross the legs in polite company.

I wanted to move the solid row of dusty plastic plants off the front of the Indonesian church dais, but was told that it couldn't be done. The same sanctuary was used for both Indonesian and English congregations, and the Indonesians didn't want their feet to be seen by the congregation. The planters stayed, but the plastic plants got washed.

How natural it seems to us to affectionately pat the head of a child. Not to parents in India, however, who consider it an unacceptable intimacy. Perhaps this began as protection of the soft spot on the head, but the gesture is also bad manners toward older children. Some believe the soul resides in the space above the head, and this area should not be intruded upon by others.

Indian women who dress with scarves over their head feel that to show the top of the head to a man outside of the family is immodest.

Saudi Arabian women either cover their entire faces with up to seven layers of a sheer black fabric, or they use the eye-slit veil of the Saudi Bedouins. Strangely, this was an ancient practice forced upon them by the Turks, who have long since dropped the custom.

This leads us to manners your mama never taught you. The *sari* of an Indian woman is rolled, folded and pinned in an elaborate manner such that it could drop at any moment if not properly done. The hidden safety pins are absolutely essential. Thus it follows that it is a terrible breach of etiquette not to return a safety pin borrowed from an Indian woman.

The Indonesian people are largely derived from five tribal groups, four of which are very gentle, polite people. (The other is not a significant portion of the population in the major cities.) Gregarious Americans, such as myself, are cautioned to tone down their emotional reactions in order to avoid misunderstandings with the very subtle Indonesians. It is advisable not to speak too loudly, not to get angry and never to put the hands on the hips, which is body language for anger.

Overt anger and other strong displays of emotion cause the Indonesians to be embarrassed, and their reaction to embarrassment is to laugh. If a westerner was angry in the first place and then got laughed at, the western reaction then is to get boiling furious. The situation quickly escalates, all because people from radically different cultures are speaking the wrong body language to one another. I can assure you that I came out of Indonesia a gentler, more reserved person than I went in.

Laughing at pain is so strange to us. At our home one day, a heavy load slipped and broke a finger of one of the men carrying it. The other three got it off the man's hand immediately. The injured man held his hand tightly at the wrist, grimacing and rocking back and forth, and he laughed. There were tears in his eyes, but he was literally laughing. After witnessing laughter at pain, it was easier to understand laughter at embarrassment.

Just a little living convinces the ex-pat that frustration with a foreign culture breeds anger, and anger fosters a heated reaction in others. Marlyn shared her experience with a representative of the São Paulo electrical power company the day he came to cut it off for non-payment.

The bill was always mailed to her husband's office, and the company always paid the bill on time. She argued angrily with the man, and he demanded to see her paid receipt.

"I don't have it . It's at the office. I'll call my husband's secretary and she will tell you that it has been paid."

She took him by the arm and rather pulled him inside, saying that he could confirm the payment by phone. He didn't want to talk to the secretary. She called anyway, and the secretary assured Marlyn that the bill had been paid. The electrician didn't care. No receipt, no power. He went outside with his clippers and cut the line.

Boy, was Marlyn mad! She got the secretary to start the process of turning the power back on, and also got a copy of the receipt. In a couple of days, the same electrician returned and spliced the wire back together.

Later, the billing problem happened again, and the same electrician came to cut the power line. Marlyn, with immense control, invited the electrician in and offered him coffee. As kindly as possible, she asked if she could call the office and verify that there had been another mistake—without mentioning *whose* mistake. She offered him a comfortable chair in the living room.

"Yes, it has happened again," she returned to say in her most cheerful manner. "This must be such a bother for you. I don't have the receipt, but the secretary has it at the office.

Could I possibly ask you not to cut the power today? I'll have the receipt here to show you tomorrow."

Well, he was really supposed to turn off the power, but if she was sure it had been paid and could have the receipt tomorrow, maybe just one day wouldn't hurt. He kept his clippers sheathed.

By the third time the same scenario occurred, they were old coffee drinking buddies. Marlyn invited him in, as if she were glad to see her friend from the power company. They had coffee in the living room, had a good laugh about the inefficiency of the bill paying process, and shook hands on his way out.

It is quite possible that the reader will not go to these specific cultures, nor need to know these particular manners and taboos. However, a sensitivity—an awareness—of the reactions to one's words and mannerisms is essential to good communication. Mother's favorite manners maxim is, after all, universal: "Good manners means making other people feel at ease."

Heimlich Who?

In developed countries we count cholesterol, take driver's education, report gas leaks and cracked sidewalks. We are preoccupied with safety and trained for disaster.

As a biology teacher and Brownie troop leader, I taught CPR and the Heimlich maneuver, using the life-size dummies from the Red Cross. Has there ever been a person in these classes who didn't secretly wish that he would be there and rush to the aid of some helpless stranger when certain death was near? In many countries, you could be the only person within a city mile who would know what to do.

So there we were at a restaurant in São Paulo, Brazil, on Saturday night. We were early, as Americans often are, and were the only diners until an elderly couple took a table on the far side of the room. Some time later, a commotion began at their table. The lady was excitedly saying to her husband in Portuguese, "Stand up! Stand up! Lift your arms!"

A waiter came quickly and began to fan him with a large burgundy-colored table napkin. The man's face was totally red and he could not utter a sound.

Our daughter was the first to be aware of the emergency. "He's choking!" Kelly said.

She and I bounded across the room, crashing our chairs backwards onto the floor. I asked the prescribed questions: "Are you okay? Can you breathe?"

(That was English, numbskull. How do you say that in Portuguese? Never mind, the guy is about to pass out. He could die before you get the expression correct.)

Since he was still standing with his arms upraised, it was easy to get behind him for the squeeze. To my surprise, though, this very slender man had distended his abdominal muscles so much in the attempt to pull in a breath that my long arms would hardly encircle him. The first squeeze was performed without my right hand locked over the left fist. It was ineffectual.

He was about to drop, but he wasn't fighting me. I got one knee up on his chair and nestled my ample bosom up tightly against the stranger's back, locked my hands and gave the sharpest, strongest pull possible. The plug of steak flew out of his windpipe and over the table. The air rushed into his lungs, and I let him gently down onto his chair. We paused a moment to ensure that all was well, and returned to our places. Let me tell you, it's hard to finish your dinner with that much adrenaline knocking around in your veins.

When the elderly couple left, the maitre d' came over to our table and asked, "What was it that to did to the gentleman to stop him from choking?"

We three explained and demonstrated the Heimlich maneuver to him and all the waiters. They had never before heard of this life-saving technique.

In the Middle East and Mediterranean, there is a popular meat variously named *swarma* or *gyro*. It is a combination of meats and spices compressed into a large, solid cylinder, mounted on a rotisserie rod to cook as it turns. As customers come for lunch, thin slices are cut from the succulent cylinder and caught into whatever bread is typical for each country.

This meat is often found mounted vertically on an electric cooker, standing on a sidewalk and tended by a man whose hands were washed at least once this week. The fragrance is wonderful as the juices begin to flow, and a line of hungry lunchers forms in front of the machine. The flies also are hungry, and there is nothing to prevent their landing on the meat for a quick bite as it rotates away from the hot coils.

142

The *swarma* cook-waiter is ever vigilant, though. With a flair, he pulls out the Pif Paf fly spray and he generously sprays the roll of meat. He smiles to the customers who will recognize that he is an excellent cook and knows the danger of flies on the meat. He continues slicing and serving, but the American who was in line for a sandwich leaves without eating. Strange.

Our American preoccupation with safety was foreign indeed to the divers at the scuba office on one of Indonesia's Thousand Islands (*Pulau Seribu*). About seven years ago, our family determined that we wanted to learn scuba. The waters all around the 13,000 islands that make up the Republic of Indonesia are rich in coral growth and a wealth of brilliantly detailed fish and every form of tropical sea life which coral development supports. If we were ever going to scuba, this was when and where. Our son, the champion swimmer, had just completed a beginning scuba course in the swimming pool of Penn State University, and I had read most of the PADI scuba school's manual. My husband and daughter had neither such advantage.

We announced ourselves as rank beginners at the hut on the beach where equipment was rented.

"Great. Do you want a guide to go with you?"

"Guide? Yes, we need a guide and, uh, some air, I reckon, and the tanks and stuff. Do you have swim fins and goggles for rent?"

We had no idea what we were doing. These scuba rental places are supposed to demand to see your beginner's scuba license which indicates that the full course has been taken and passed with tests on paper and in the water. They knew that three of us had never seen the equipment up close, and they started passing out gear and helping us suit up.

A skinny but fit Indonesian young man in a badly torn nylon wet suit motioned for us to follow him, and we walked into the shallows like four mechanical ducks behind the wrong mother. He showed us how to fit the mouthpieces

First Time to Scuba

into our faces and a couple of things about how they work, and we breathed under water and checked the seal around our goggles. Next he showed us the hand signals for "up," "down," and "my air is blocked off and I'm going to die."

And that was it. We pushed off into Jacques Cousteau Land for the most exciting ride of our lives.

Mothers, don't ever take off on a new, potentially dangerous sport with your spouse and all your progeny at once. It's scary. You could all die in one "swell foop."

But then I realized that I had been stiff with fear for the first fifteen minutes and the very people for whom I was so afraid were having the times of their lives. The ocean life was indescribably beautiful. I was doing something I had dreamed of since seeing it on TV as a child, and the reality was even better than the dream. What a rush!

The scuba equipment hut had only enough for the guide and three divers, which was okay the first day because I was being sick back in the hotel room. On the second day, our son Quinn graciously insisted that I take his equipment and he would just get fins and paddle along on the surface above us.

We were at a depth of about thirty feet when my husband felt a tap on his shoulder. It was Quinn, signaling that he wanted a breath of air from his father. And although Darrel had never had that lesson, he passed him the mouthpiece. Quinn breathed twice, and Darrel was able to re-insert, purge the water from the mouthpiece, and resume breathing without a problem. Quinn swam around for a while, got another charge of air, and eventually went back up to the surface.

We had all done five or ten dives each by the time we tried to rent equipment from a registered PADI company in Hawaii. They said, in essence, "No way." We spent our Hawaiian vacation getting up before dawn for study, homework, classes, written tests, practical submerged experience and tests in the water. We left with a fresh set of Open Water Diver certificates, although we had not dived the waters we had hoped to see. We've never regretted it.

Ex-pats at Gunpoint

"What's so amusing about being held at gunpoint over-seas?" you might ask. "I could stay in my own country and get robbed." This is true. Perhaps by reading of the experiences of others, though, you will avoid being a victim of the same set-up. Besides, some stories are just too good not to be told.

Our Swiss friend, Werner, was driving in broad daylight down Avenida Paulista, the widest, richest street in Brazil, which is lined with banks. At a traffic light, a man entered his car on the passenger side and held a gun to Werner's head and told him to drive. Werner drove. The man had just robbed a bank and was having problems with the getaway. The details are unclear, since Werner didn't ask a lot of questions. After a few blocks, the guy sprang out and ran off, leaving a very shaky young man glad to be returning to his family that night. He doesn't forget to lock his car door any more.

Some people just don't deserve to get robbed. Take Dr. Sloan, for example. He is a person in whom there is no guile, the superintendent of a Christian school in a metropolis in South America. Dr. Sloan was driving on the city's perimeter highway when a truck with two men waved him down. He pulled to the side, and the men convinced him that his car was spewing fumes out the back and something was badly wrong. They were mechanics, they said, and offered to help. They lifted the hood with his permission. The mechanics monkeyed around under the hood for a while, and said they had found the problem. Again with his permission, they removed the offending part and left to get a replacement for it. After Dr. Sloan had waited by the busy highway for a while, unable now to start his engine, the two men returned in their truck with a part which they quickly put in. The car started up, and sounded good.

Dr. Sloan appreciated their help, and asked how much he owed them. They were willing to accept the equivalent of about two hundred dollars. Dr. Sloan doesn't walk around with that much cash. The mechanics would take a check, but Dr. Sloan didn't have his checkbook with him. The mechanics agreed to follow Dr. Sloan back to the Christian school, where the secretary would prepare a check on the school's account.

At the school, one of the mechanics waited in the office while the other sat in the truck. The secretary had gotten the name to whom the check should be made, and left the outer office. It was taking too long to make out the check, so Dr. Sloan tried to make small talk with the mechanic and offered him coffee. There was some problem with the computer that prints up the checks, he said, wondering why the mechanic was getting sweaty and nervous. Suddenly the mechanic said he had to go out to the truck and tell his friend something, but he got in the truck and drove away very fast. Just then the secretary came in with the check for two hundred dollars worth of pesos, but the men were gone. Looking back over the whole event, Dr. Sloan realized that it had all been a scam operation. They had left because they thought Dr. Sloan was stalling until the police arrived to take them away. But until that moment, he had never guessed that they were thieves.

While I don't have percentage figures or bar graphs on this, it is fairly certain that most confrontational robberies happen on the sidewalk. We who live in places where street robberies happen frequently, develop a jewelry wardrobe for which ten dollars per item is a high value, and a five-dollar watch with a plastic band gets compliments from the ladies at tea. I used to have a two dollar golden necklace which my friends and language professor suggested I not wear on the street because it looked like real gold. In time, it tarnished enough that it was safe to wear.

In Mexico City, a woman was wearing a multiple chain necklace which appeared to be gold but was not. An attractive young man in good clothes was walking toward her on the sidewalk. Just as he passed her, he reached out and grabbed the necklace to break it off her neck. She said later that she couldn't imagine why she reacted the way she did, but in the few seconds that he was pulling on her necklace, she noticed that he also wore a necklace and she grabbed hold of it. Both necklaces broke and the young robber ran away with her fake and she stood there holding his solid gold chain in her hand!

It was also in Mexico City that a lady, whom I shall call Denise, went to her bank to cash a check. She had to go inside the bank and wait in line. Receiving the stack of peso bills, she started to shove the cash into her purse and leave, when the gentleman behind her in line offered her a white envelope and insisted that she put her cash in the envelope before putting it in her purse. It was safer that way, he said. He was very polite, well dressed, and obviously a kind and caring person. She thanked him profusely, used the envelope, and left the bank.

Denise drove straight home. As she arrived in front of her house, she noticed for the first time that she had been followed. Denise emerged from her car, and the kind gentleman from the bank got out of his car and pulled a gun on her.

"Give me the envelope," he demanded, holding the gun in line with her heart. Confused, frightened, and offended by this stranger whom she had just been thanking for his thoughtfulness, Denise reached into her purse, pulled out the white envelope, and handed it to him. He drove off quickly and she ran into the house.

It happened that her husband was home, and she rushed to tell him, crying and almost shouting, what had happened. She was talking with her hands, and when she got to the part about handing the robber the envelope, she opened her purse and, in fact, pulled out a white envelope for the second time. Lo and behold, it was the envelope containing the stack of bills! So what had she just given the robber in front of her house? It was then that Denise remembered that as she had left the house to do her errands that morning, she had modestly enclosed a feminine sanitary napkin inside a white envelope. And that was what the robber had taken from her at gunpoint!

In Bogatá, Colombia, a resident told of her mother's experience while walking on the sidewalk in a busy, prosperous shopping area. Being a careful person, the mother was holding her purse in the "football carry" position, as is recommended. That way, it isn't strapped to your body if someone is determined to get it. A young man paused and asked her directions to a certain address. They discussed the best way to get there for just a moment, and then they parted in opposite ways. As she walked off, she noticed that her purse seemed heavier somehow. To her amazement, she was no longer carrying her purse at all. She now had, safely cradled in her arm, a papaya wrapped in newspaper! She had absolutely no idea when or how the transfer had happened. Obviously, this guy was wasting his time doing petty thievery. He should be performing magic acts on stage.

On a beautiful spring morning in San Isidro, a residential suburb of Buenos Aires, Karen and Jennifer went to the town plaza to see what was being sold, painted, sung and eaten at the impromptu "fair." They were walking past the stalls of crafts and antiques, chatting and enjoying the weather, when a thief ripped Jennifer's Rolex watch off her wrist and ran through the crowd. They shouted and tried to follow, but he was getting away toward the commuter train station a few blocks away. The women ran to Karen's car and dashed to a little police station to ask for help. There was no police car at the station at the moment, but Karen said they could go in her car. *All* the police hopped into the car, leaving no room for the women, the only ones who could identify the thief and legally drive the car.

Some of the policemen got out and the two women got in, and the carload raced for the train station. The train pulled out toward Accasusso just as the car arrived. Passersby confirmed that the man they described got on the train in an urgent rush.

Everyone piled back into the car after leaving a message with the train office attendant to call ahead and have the man apprehended. I wish I could tell you that the Keystone Kops caught their man and the watch was returned, but he apparently jumped off the moving train before the next stop. The watch probably joined its sisters in the window of one of the stores downtown that advertises "previously owned" Rolexes.

Mr. Kraus, executive of a German manufacturer doing business in Chile, checked out of his hotel in Santiago early one morning. He had to visit several sites in other cities during the day, so he had hired a car and driver. His bags were loaded into the car in the most routine fashion and the trip began.

Arriving at the first site, he attempted to retrieve the necessary paperwork from his briefcase in the trunk. Instead, he found the briefcase filled with $40,000 in U.S. cash. Oh, darn the bad luck! It was, in fact, very bad luck to have someone else's $40,000 in a small village in Chile when he was completely identifiable and traceable. And someone else had Mr. Kraus' passport, itinerary details, as well as the contracts and paper trail which he now needed.

There was no time to go back. He didn't even call back. Was he going to tell a hotel clerk in Santiago that he was on a back road in Chile with $40,000 cash? He wasn't about to give it up to Chilean police, either. He needed to exchange it for his own paperwork and just assume the briefcase belonged to a person making a generous donation to an orphanage or his mother's pension fund.

What Mr. Kraus did, in fact, was to continue his schedule of site visits, a lunch meeting, and appointments through several villages. He left the briefcase in the trunk without mentioning the little complication even to his driver.

When he arrived that night as planned at the hotel in San Fernando, Chile, two men were waiting for him outside. They emerged from a black car, scanning the area from behind dark glasses.

"I believe our briefcases were accidentally exchanged," one of them said without introduction.

Mr. Kraus agreed, and handed over the briefcase identical to his except for the contents. He received his case, and the two returned to their car. After they had time to check the cash, they drove away. By then, Mr. Kraus was checking into the hotel, another routine day on the road behind him.

A few years ago, an American family we shall call the Maxwells, living in São Paulo, Brazil, were delighted to learn that Mrs. Maxwell's mother was coming for a visit. The children were so happy to see Grandmother! Mr. Maxwell arranged some vacation time away from the U.S. Consulate, and the family planned a road trip to take Grandmother to see a small part of the Brazilian countryside.

First they would drive to the cool mountain area of Campos do Jordão and spend the first night there. Then they would angle up to Belo Horizonte, which means "beautiful horizon." The gold leaf covered cathedrals of Ouro Preto had to be included in that area, and no one should leave Brazil without seeing Rio de Janeiro. This was going to be such fun.

Grandmother arrived, and after resting from the all night flight, she was ready to push off on the great adventure.

Campos do Jordão, with its fake German-ness and its chocolate candy for tourists, was green and peaceful. The second day, the family drove all the way to Belo Horizonte. On the third day they were further north and in a very isolated area when, as they were stopped for a picnic lunch, Grandmother had a massive heart attack and died.

In Brazil, embalming is rare and burial must be within twenty-four hours. That's the law. And embalming is only done, they were told, in São Paulo. Furthermore, there is a very lengthy process to get the paperwork necessary to have a body shipped home. It takes weeks, and involves police investigation of the slightest irregularity.

Mr. and Mrs. Maxwell decided that they could not risk getting involved with the local police. The most logical thing to do was to load up and drive night and day until they got to the American Consulate in São Paulo.

The Maxwells could not bear the thought of riding all those hours with Grandmother propped up in the back seat. The children were already near hysteria. Suitcases were removed from the trunk and baggage shifted around until they could put Grandmother to rest in the trunk. The Maxwells started the long drive home with the kids sniveling in the back seat.

You can only drive so long before someone has to go to the bathroom. Everyone was hungry, too, and even lesser highways in Brazil have *churrascarias* every few miles. Spotting a particularly appealing restaurant, they parked in the lot and went in for a full meal and rest stop.

When they returned to the lot after dinner, though, the car was missing! Frantically they searched, but the car was gone. Now they had to call the police, and it was also time to call the American Consulate. Everyone got involved, but the stolen car was never found. Not a piece, not a suitcase, and not Grandmother.

Stealing Grandmother

If it was difficult to process papers to have a body embalmed and exported to the home country, just imagine what it was like to declare dead a woman that you can't find. It isn't at all legal to have a person enter on a tourist visa and disappear. Mr. Maxwell claimed that his mother-in-law died in the countryside, but only the immediate family members were witnesses. There was no body, no police report, no death certificate. It was months before the Consulate could legally lay Grandmother to rest, wherever she may be. She, the car, and the suitcases were never found.

Jean was pleased to have the girlfriend of her son visit the family in São Paulo. The two ladies decided to drive to Rio de Janeiro and enjoy this beautiful city together. It's about an eight hour road trip, but not bad if you dodge the trucks and don't get lost in the potholes.

They laughed and talked along the way, sometimes playing the radio and sometimes listening to the tapes they had brought. This was great fun.

Eventually, they stopped and went into a restaurant, discovering to their dismay that they had walked in on an armed robbery. The robbers turned on them and demanded that Jean give them her car. Ever the calm and logical one, Jean replied in Portuguese, "You may take the car, but we are on a trip to Rio. Please let us keep our suitcases."

The robbers agreed, and they went with Jean and the young lady and held the gun on them while they hauled their luggage out of the car.

One of the robbers got the car key from Jean, and attempted to start the car. Since Jean's husband was an executive of an American-based car company, she had the latest and best of their locally made cars. The car had an automatic steering wheel locking device which the robber did not understand. Under threat of being shot, she showed him how to free the steering wheel and start the car.

"But hey, what's this?" he countered, again feeling tricked. "Where's the gear shift?"

"It's an automatic transmission. The lever is up here, behind the steering wheel. You just put it in 'reverse' to get it out of the parking space, then up to 'drive,' " she explained. "I've never driven a car like this. Show me," he said. And so Jean not only had to give her car to the robbers, but she had to teach them how to drive it away.

Another dear friend whose husband is an automobile company executive in South America has been car-jacked twice. These are not funny stories—just a gun to her head and the knowledge that life may be over any minute. Linda stayed calm and the robbers stole the car and released her without physical injury. Now she is trying to get the company to issue her an old car, maybe something that runs well but has a couple of dents. The company cannot do that, however, because her husband is a senior executive. She has to have a new car. Have we just invented Catch 23?

Linda also has the distinction of being involved in the most unlikely hold-up among the residents of her community. A few years ago, in the same South American city, she was in dire straits with a gastro-intestinal ailment. The only doctor she had a patient relationship with was a gynecologist-obstetrition. She entered the office and saw that today it was filled with pregnant women and their husbands. Too miserable to leave, desperately needing attention, she registered and took a seat to wait.

Into the waiting room burst a madman with a gun, waving the weapon and shouting in Portuguese. He found the doctor and nurses and shouted at them for a while, threatening to kill them all. Linda was never sure exactly what he wanted, because doctors don't normally keep cash around. No one ever saw drugs or medicines be given to him. He just kept screaming in Portuguese and waving that gun around.

The doctor tried to keep everyone calm, saying the gun wasn't loaded and the man wasn't really going to hurt anyone. In fact, it came out later that the criminal had escaped from either a prison or mental institution and was already a murderer.

The madman rounded up all the patients and their husbands and pushed the whole bunch into a small ladies' room down the hall. They were so crowded that people were standing on the toilets, smushed up against one another, warned to stay there or die.

After about two hours, police opened the door and let them out. The severity of Linda's disease had passed over, and she returned home without treatment. Those doctor's office waits can be awful.

Our employers often tell us that we have no basis for worry or complaint; that you are as likely to be mugged in your home country. Maybe so, but somehow it's different when you are far, far from home, the thief is yelling in another language, and he considers you a rich foreigner who deserves to be robbed. There is a special place in our hearts for those who have been through what we all fear.

Sex in the Afternoon

I should have guessed something was up just by the tone of voice Teresa used. She had called to invite me to Suzanna's farewell party. Of course, I was glad to go. Suzanna and I had worked together on committees for a couple of years, and her husband was being transferred to the Orient. I didn't know the hostess Teresa at all, but Suzanna had given her my name for the guest list. Teresa was inviting about fifty ladies for a *paella* lunch at her apartment, and I do love *paella*. But then her voice changed—became sort of conspiratorial—and she said something like, "You do like to have a good time, don't you? Some people don't know how to have fun." So I figured that we were going to hold a kangaroo court and give Suzanna some gag gifts and giggle a lot. I assured Teresa that I enjoy a good laugh.

It was a beautiful apartment. We were on the twentieth floor in a group of apartment buildings with a guarded entrance and lush landscaping. There must have been at least fifty ladies chattering in Spanish, Portuguese, and English. I didn't know most of them, but I enjoyed slaughtering all three languages with equanimity.

The day was bright and hot, nearing Christmas in the tropics, so I spent a lot of time on the little balcony off the living room appreciating the breeze and the distant view. Sangria and wine were being served, which didn't make me any cooler.

The *paella* was probably the best I have ever had. Then there were two or three desserts and strong Brazilian coffee in beautiful little cups. By this time, we had been there for about three hours, and I was ready to get my purse and start my creep to the door.

But the hostess called us in from the patio and pulled the heavy living room curtains, which made the room stifling. At that moment the strangest feeling came over me that we were going to participate in something that we wouldn't want the children to see. Now I had been out on the balcony and I knew there wasn't another building anywhere around for miles, so drawing the drapes was unnecessary. It looked as if we were setting the stage for mischief.

What really bothered me was the way these nice ladies started cackling and gleaming. I asked what was happening. One woman said, "Didn't you know?" and Teresa said, "Papai Noel is coming." Again, it was the tone that bothered me.

Someone in the corner started some holly, jolly Christmas music and, sure enough, Papai Noel entered from the kitchen area. Wearing the typical red Santa suit and hat, shiny black plastic boots, and a fake white synthetic beard, he carried a handful of red rosebuds. You could tell there was a swarthy young man under the Santa suit.

He walked around the room and handed the rosebuds to ladies at random. I got one, since I was sitting right on the front row. The living room had two major sitting areas, so Papai Noel moved with the music to the other side and gave a rose to a seventy-ish lady who was sitting rather upright on the big sofa. She must have had a headache, because she didn't even smile at him.

He started to leave the room, but the hostess called loudly to him, "Hey, where are you going?"

"Well, I came and gave out the roses. I was going to leave now," he replied.

"Not yet. Come on, stay for the party," she said, invitingly.

Then the person in the corner stopped the jolly Christmas music and put on a throbbing bump and grind and the hostess and Santa Claus started doing the *lambada* right there in the darkened living room. Santa was working up a sweat, so he pulled off the Christmas hat and tossed it to someone sitting cross-legged in the floor and kept dancing. Now with the kind of dance he was doing, and the way his body was moving, he was getting warmer all the time. So he started dancing around the circle of women and motioning to them that they should help him get out of his hot costume. First the beard, then the belt, then the tunic came off, and he wasn't wearing a shirt. The women were undressing him as he continued to dance, and he wasn't cooling off a bit.

The other guests seemed to know the correct way to do this, because I noticed that they were careful never to actually touch the man. In slipping off the suspenders, for example, one of the guests used a pencil rather than touching his lithe, brown, gyrating body. I believe it was at this point that another one of the women danced with him and I felt like I wasn't supposed to be watching this. Or maybe that was after he extended his foot into a woman's lap, encouraging her to pull the boot off, and she eventually did so with some fairly suggestive tugs.

My mind was racing. I didn't want to be here. Why did they invite me to something like this? Didn't they realize, whatever my personal beliefs and motives may be, that I, a church organist, would be out of place at a party with a male stripper? Indignant and embarrassed, I was looking for a chance to get out of there, but didn't want to cross the dance floor and draw attention to myself. Every time I looked toward the door across the circle of titillated women vibrating with the music, my eyes met the eyes of Anna, whom I had been trying to Lead to the Lord.

I had to leave. Everything I had ever said to her would be a sham if I stayed in that room. Suddenly my opportunity came. The stripper, now wearing skin-tight black leotards, danced into the other sitting area of the living room where the elderly lady looked severely put upon, and I dashed for the door. Anna followed me to the elevator, looking a bit

Papai Noel Gets Hot

apologetic. She left the apartment door open a bit so it wouldn't lock behind her, and I waited an eternity for the elevator to rise to the twentieth floor.

"It's going to be all right," Anna was assuring me. "He isn't going to take everything off." As I entered the elevator, turned around, and looked back, the hard, dark, writhing young man was on the floor in front of a woman who was peeling off the black leotard. There was still a tiny black stretch of fabric covering his most intimate parts.

I escaped into the blazing sunlight and threw myself into the traffic toward the city. It took me several miles to realize that I was really irritated about the whole experience, not the least because it wasn't sexually stimulating to me. The guy was, in my daughter's terms, a "hunk." Was I that old? Had I lost it all?

Distancing myself from the experience, my mind reached toward home and husband, and the love for my middle-aged businessman flowed over me like a warm, gentle river. No, I hadn't lost it all. And thank God, neither had he.

Daddy's Gift

My father, whom I still and always will call "Daddy," came down to Brazil for a three week visit. He was recuperating from major surgery, so we planned little excursions of one or two hours each day. Since São Paulo is not the jiving tourist city that Rio de Janeiro is, I feared he might see its crowded, ugly side and not appreciate its more favorable assets.

I need not have worried. Within a few days he had picked up a refrain of "Eva-body oughta come to Brazil." We never shopped, he didn't care to eat meals in our many restaurants, and he didn't have enough art background to enjoy the museums. What impressed Daddy, then?

He was amazed at the millions of people and the crazy traffic. When we were out in the car, he gave a running monologue of what the other drivers were doing, like a sportscaster at a world cup game. He took countless pictures of the tall buildings, and from the top of the Hilton we photographed the city center. Every postcard sent home was of the skyscrapers.

Riding the subway was a delight, and walking the streets of the Japanese section, Liberdade, amazed him. On Avenida Paulista he was fascinated with how many city buses lined up at once during the rush hour. We even went to the center island and took pictures of them, and returned another day to videotape them for the folks back home. Puzzled natives watched us, trying to determine what there was to tape.

Daddy had visited many big cities, but this was the best of all. He was thrilled with the very things I disliked most about São Paulo: crowds, traffic, tall buildings, crazy drivers, and long rows of city buses.

Daddy returned to Alabama, but he left a wonderful gift behind. When I look at the buildings and buses and get bogged in traffic now I chuckle, thinking, "Daddy would really love this."

Thanks, Daddy. São Paulo looks even better through your eyes.

The Simi Shrimp Dinner

Burley Reese was a great big bear of a man, an Australian banker in Singapore. He and his wife loved to sail, so they devised a fantastic vacation plan with two other sailing couples: they would fly from Singapore, jointly rent a sailboat in Turkey, and cruise the Greek islands for several weeks.

As the date approached, they feared the whole trip would be canceled because the Gulf War broke out. Burley made desperate calls to ensure that their reservations would be held. He needn't have worried. Their hosts didn't know there was a war on. If they had been anxious to go before, they were now in a fine state of ecstasy.

Finally the big day came, and the three couples flew to the cerulean waters for the most incredibly beautiful sailing experience of their lives.

One particular experience Burley liked to tell had to do with hostilities between the Turks and the Greeks, and the night they moored at the Greek island of Simi, practically "spitting distance" from the Turkish coast.

Sailing from Turkey on a boat of Turkish ownership, they had flown a small Turkish flag on the mast of the boat. As they crossed into Greek waters, they should have put a Greek flag on the mast. Since the sailboat was registered in Turkey, the Turkish flag now should have been aft of the boat. Desiring to show that the occupants were all Australian, they also rigged on Australian flag on one side.

For days, the crew had been talking about how they were going to eat some of the famous Simi shrimp when they got to the island. Smoothly the boat slid into port and the crew tied her down and started to clean up for dinner. They could hardly wait.

But Greek sailors on the boat moored beside theirs started yelling at them. The Australians had no idea what the Greeks were saying, but the Greeks were furious. One of the Australians responded by shouting a few choice expressions, and the situation began to heat up. The wives feared that their husbands were in danger.

The three wives literally pulled the two hotter-headed husbands off the boat to take a walk on the beach and work off the steam. Burley, the enormous but calm one, stayed with the boat.

When the beach walkers returned, the designated guard was gone. In a panic, they called Burley and looked all about for him.

Drawn to the merry ruckus in the boat to their side, they found Burley drinking beer with the Greek sailors. Everyone was in a great mood. The Greeks, reading the flag positions and noting that the Greek flag was not on top while in Greek waters, thought the Australians were Turks. They weren't about to let a load of disrespectful Turks berth beside them. Australians, however, were fine.

By now, our friends were very hungry for those Simi shrimp, and they had the name of a restaurant down the beach where the best were to be found. They invited the Greek sailors to come along to dinner with them, and they all took off walking together.

The restaurant was a beach-weathered, rustic place run by two generations of a family: the middle-aged parents, their adult daughter and her husband. The folksy, hospitable atmosphere floated on Papa's wine, made out back and served exclusively in their restaurant. It wasn't bad, and the Simi shrimp were excellent. The two crews could hardly communicate with one another, but they ate shrimp, drank Papa's wine, and roared for hours.

One of the Australians, perhaps the one who started off with the Greek crew's beer, was "deep in his cups." He proposed marriage to the waitress with his own wife by his side and the waitress' husband also serving the table. No one took him seriously, but it was time to leave.

They called for the bill. It was so low that the group left a tip amounting to fifty percent of the bill. They pushed up from the table and staggered down the beach toward the boat, singing and laughing, stumbling in the sand. The waitress came running behind them, breathlessly protesting that they had left too much money.

"No, no, that's what we intended. The food was great. Keep it all," Burley jovially insisted.

"Well, then, at least take another bottle of me papa's wine."

It was one of the finest nights of their lives.

The Tomb of Queen Nefertiti

Darrel and his co-worker Bruce had a week-end free during their business trip to Cairo, and were able to arrange a hired car with driver and guide for only twenty-five dollars for the whole day. The guide, Ismael, was a particularly enthusiastic fellow. He wanted to show them everything possible. He recommended the pyramid in which Queen Nefertiti had been buried, with stops at the papyrus factory, perfume maker, and textile factory. Guides always get a percentage of what the tourists spend, so the extra stops were expected.

Arriving at the site not distant from Gaza, they found the three-tiered earth and rock pyramid among the ruins of its former city. Ismael was quite insistent that he take Darrel and Bruce down to the bottom of the pyramid, but there was an electrical power outage that day. The guard on duty at the entrance had no flashlight, so Ismael scouted around until he was able to borrow a Bic cigarette lighter from a different guard. This was great. They could go down after all.

Bending almost double to enter the one meter square opening, the men found a smooth, ladder-like ramp descending at about a thirty degree angle. Saving the lighter for the deeper reaches, they went single file like Mumbo, Jumbo and Dumbo. Holding onto the belt loop of each one in front, they scuffled down into the void.

The chamber at the bottom was a large square room in which they were able to stand up, but once standing, they could no longer see up the ramp to the outside. It was black as the inside of a whale's belly, and absolutely quiet.

Ismael lit the Bic and led them into a wide passageway off the right side of the first chamber. They were able to stand as they walked, but Ismael cautioned them to stay to the right because there was a deep pit somewhere on the left.

Down this passageway they went to another chamber in which Queen Nefertiti's sarcophagus lay open, her mummified body having been removed. Painted on all the walls and ceiling were fascinating pictographs and hieroglyphics, which Ismael was eager to explain. Raising the Bic to the ceiling, he was excitedly interpreting the signs when the plastic lighter underwent a catastrophic melt-down. Hot plastic and metal showered to the floor and the room was plunged into total darkness.

The guide yelped when the lighter burned his hand, but the cry bounced back to the three men from the tomb's stone walls. No matter how wide open their eyes stretched, only deepest black was upon them. The enormity of the situation broke over the group. They were under some thirty meters of dirt and rocks. Absolutely the only thing they could see was that the tour was over.

Groping to find the way out of the sarcophagus room, they formed up in train as before and felt their way back with their left shoulders lightly brushing the wall. One step too far to the right lay death in the dark.

Arriving at the opening to the first chamber, the guide remembered to turn left to find the ramp upwards. They saw no light. All three men waved their hands against the wall as if trying to find a light switch in the night. The ramp had to be there somewhere. Surely they were back in the first chamber, not lost in some side room along the way.

At last one of them realized that the ramp entered the chamber at the bottom of its wall, not at eye level. They all bent down and crawled around until one found diffuse light at the end of the fifty meter ramp. Looking up the straight shaft, an image was burned forever into their memories: the black silhouette of a soldier sitting across the entrance, knees propped up, smoking a cigarette, with the brilliant desert light behind him. They had found the way out.

Did I Just Kiss the Waiter?

Our company's branch in Buenos Aires, Argentina, had rented the big tent of an amusement park for the Christmas party. Hundreds of employees and their spouses were present. Those of our department began to spot each other and tried to greet and congregate in one area.

In Argentina, women greet each other by kissing. Actually, their cheeks lightly touch, and the two ladies make a tiny kissy noise. Likewise, the ladies offer the little kiss to all the gentlemen. The men give each other an *abrazo*, which is a simultaneous handshake and sideways back slap. It's all very congenial, but an essential social exchange.

So we were under the big top with a sea of round tables and folding chairs set up, leaving precious little space for people to get their cheeks together and then back up for someone else. We were stumbling over chairs and being very merry, especially since Darrel and I were just trying to get the hang of this kind of greeting. It didn't feel natural yet.

At least one lady stuck out her cheek and Darrel took about two seconds to realize he was supposed to kiss it. But we weren't total klutzes, and we did like the people he worked with.

First thing on Monday morning, one of the young officers came into Darrel's office and closed the door behind him. He was very sober.

"Have you been pleased with my work?" he asked.

Caught off guard by the question, Darrel assured him he was.

The young man fished around again, trying to discover what he had done wrong or wasn't doing right.

Darrel was mystified. "What's the matter, Carlos? Why do you ask?"

"Why didn't you kiss my wife at the Christmas party Saturday? You kissed all the other ladies, but not my wife." Somehow, in the dance of the folding chairs, Angelina had been omitted. Carlos thought this was a sign that his career was going down the drain with the new boss.

To this day, when we return to Argentina, Angelina gets an extra-warm greeting. This incident has helped to teach us that the little kisses are not optional.

Our children were eleven and fourteen when we moved to Argentina. You might think that they would be shy about giving the little kisses, *besos*, but not so. They fell right in line.

A few years later we were living in Brazil where the ritual gets more complicated. Two kisses are normally given, one on each cheek. If one of the persons is a single woman, a third kiss is given as a wish for her to be married. That's left, right, left. Imagine a group of eight or ten people getting together. Kissy, kissy, left-right, left-right-left. Some may be from other countries and not like the procedure, but leaving out one person makes others wonder why. It's better to include everyone.

You get used to it such that your own family back home seems cold when they greet you with a "hi." Is that all? I want a warm touch, you think.

Soon after I returned to Brazil from putting our daughter in college, she called home sounding on the very brink of tears. "No one kisses here, Mom. I need a hug."

You begin to see now how it all happened. We were living in Argentina, and there was to be a client dinner that night at the home of Darrel's senior, a Swiss-German married to Swiss-French. Normally, I would have received a list of the guests giving the names of both husband and wife, and maybe their nationality. But the list never happened.

Darrel was coming to the dinner from the office, and I would meet him from the house.

The invitation was for seven thirty, although Argentines always come late. The host couple, being Swiss, never vary more than thirty seconds from the invitation time. I aimed for the correct time, but arrived ten minutes late. All the guests were already there. All were Europeans except us.

Argentines kiss once, French twice, Swiss twice, Germans once or twice?—what language are we speaking tonight? *Uh-oh, I'm not catching the names.* And Darrel was embarrassed that I was coming in late, but hey! I didn't know the guests weren't Argentines. I thought I was early! I was trying not to look rattled, but it was a first class ninny act.

Backing out of the tight circle, I slid past a couple of the ladies whom I had already kissed, I think, and retreated sideways toward a gentleman in a nice black suit that I hadn't noticed before. Had we already been introduced, or was he in line to be kissed next? Which wife went with which husband? He spoke in Argentine Spanish. He looked the most disapproving of all the guests. I didn't reply to his Spanish, because it took me a couple of seconds for his words to sink in.

"What will you have, señora?"

Oh, no. I think he's a waiter.

Somehow we got the evening on track, and it was a lovely dinner. I hobbled through and got to bed by midnight, another mid-week business dinner done.

But at about three a.m. I woke up from a deep sleep with a horrible thought. I sat up in bed with a cold sweat on my brow, eyes wide open in the dark. *Did I just kiss the waiter?*

I still don't know, and I'll never know. I probably made an absolute fool of myself.

Did I Just Kiss the Waiter?

That's one of the risks of living the way we do. By the time you learn your way around in one culture and language, you move to another.

It's never dull.

About the Author

Born and reared in Atmore, Alabama, Lee Carver had never moved until going off to college. Graduating with a double major in biology and chemistry plus a minor in French, she accepted a full scholarship for a Ph.D. in biochemistry and expected to spend the rest of her life in a lab. Pushed into a blind date with Darrel Carver, she married him four months later and soon left academia.

The family budded during Darrel's years as a Navy pilot, and grew during his international business career. With son Quinn and daughter Kelly, they have lived in eight of the United States and five foreign countries. Now empty-nesters, the Carvers live at the present in São Paulo, Brazil, where the wonderful adventure continues.

About the Artist

Quinn Carver, sometime freelance graphic artist, has loaned his creative genius to the cartoons found herein. Quinn's drawings and swim records have decorated four nations. Graduates in biology from Penn State University, he and his lovely wife still make their home near its village.

Quinn is president of Techkor Andromechanics, where he is working on the invention of a myoelectric prosthetic hand.

Index of Illustrations